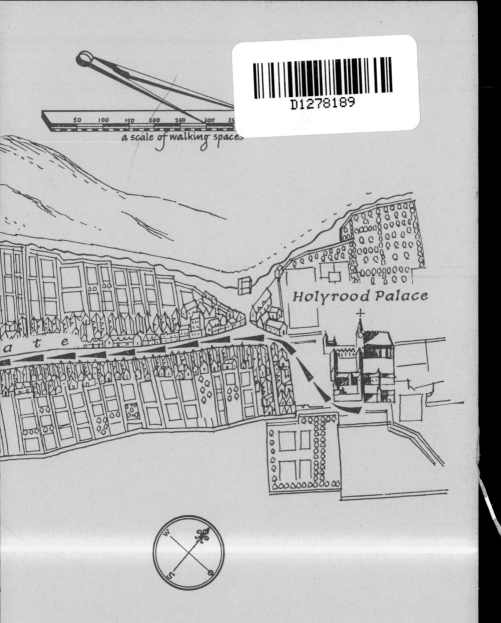

a scale of walking spaces

Holyrood Palace

The Route
aken by the Murderers

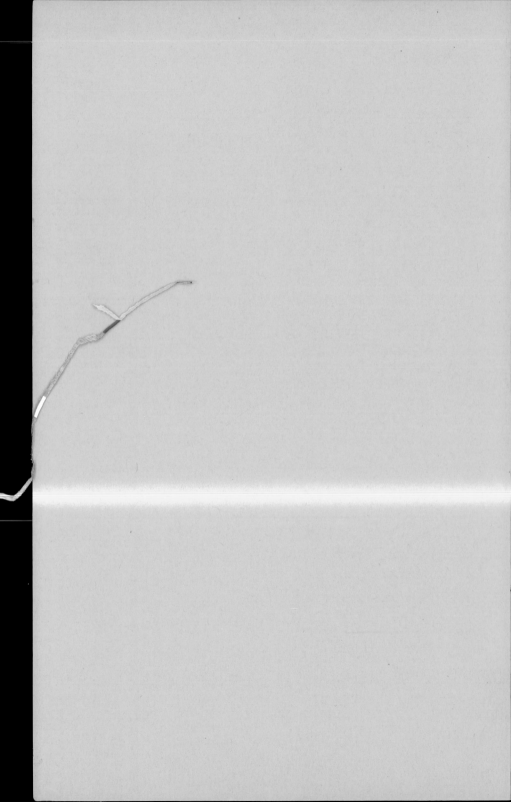

The Crime of Mary Stuart

By the same author
THE TWELVE DAYS

New Hanover County Public Library
Main Library
1/3/2012

Thank you for using self-checkout!

**********8442

34200000665006 (BC): The crime of Mary
Stuart.
Date Due: 01/24/2012 11:59:00 PM

Monday and Tuesday 9 A.M to 8 P.M.
Wednesday and Thursday 9 A.M. to 6 P.M.
Friday and Saturday 9 A.M. to 5 P.M.
Telephone Renewals: 910-798-6320
Website: www.nhclibrary.org
Checked Out / # Not Checked Out
1 / 1

Mary, Queen of Scots

Artist unknown

GEORGE MALCOLM THOMSON

The Crime of Mary Stuart

New York : *1967*
E. P. DUTTON & CO., INC.

Strike or be stricken, strike or be stricken

Queen Elizabeth the First

Contents

Illustrations

The portrait of Darnley is reproduced by gracious permission of Her
Majesty the Queen. The portrait of Mary Stuart is in the ownership of
the Glasgow Art Gallery and Museum, and the portraits of the Earl of
Bothwell and the Earl of Moray are the copyright of the Scottish National
Portrait Gallery. These are thanked for their permission to reproduce.
The Clouet painting of Diane de Poitiers is from the Radio Times Hulton
Picture Library.

Acknowledgements

I ACKNOWLEDGE WITH GRATITUDE the courteous help I have received in preparing this book from the officials of the National Library of Scotland, the Register House, Edinburgh, the Central Public Library, Edinburgh, the Huntly House Museum, Canongate, Edinburgh, and also from the explosives experts of the Home Office and the Institution of Royal Engineers, Chatham. It need not be said that none of these authorities has any responsibility for statements I have made or conclusions I have reached. I should also acknowledge my debt to Mr. Armstrong Davison's careful analysis of 'The Casket Letters' in his book of that name. Although I have not been able to accept all his findings, I have derived real benefit from his meticulous examination and his original views.

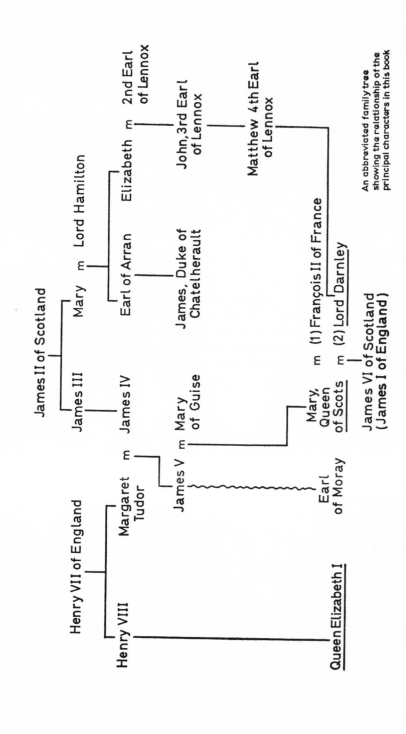

An abbreviated family tree showing the relationship of the principal characters in this book

The Crime of Mary Stuart

The Crime

Not long after two o'clock in the morning of Monday, February 10, 1567, Mrs. Barbara Martin, awakened by some noise, went to the window of her house in Blackfriars' Wynd, Edinburgh. This was a narrow, steep lane sloping downhill from the High Street towards the south to cross the Cowgate. In it were some substantial town houses of the gentry. For example, just opposite Mrs. Martin was the lodging of the Master of Maxwell. Not far away was the mansion of the Earl of Morton, who, during the minority of his nephew, the Earl of Angus, was the effective head of the powerful Douglas connection.

Mrs. Martin claimed later, on oath, that she heard thirteen men emerge from Friars' Gate, the entrance to a disused church and monastic buildings. They made their way up the Wynd towards the south in the direction of the Town Wall. Shortly afterwards there was a loud explosion. Then eleven men, two of whom wore clothing of a light colour, passed down the alley in the opposite direction and hurried towards the centre of the town. She called out to them, 'Traitors, you have been at some evil turn!'

The night was dark; the new moon would not appear for another four hours. Thin snow lying on the street may have given some reflected light. Even so, Mrs. Martin's estimate of the number of men she saw might be regarded with suspicion; however, it is exactly corroborated by another piece of evidence.

On the opposite side of Blackfriars' Wynd, Mrs. Mary Crockett, wife of John Stirling, the Archbishop of St. Andrew's servant, was fast asleep that night between the twins when she was awakened by the explosion. Thinking that it came from the house over her head (where the Master of Maxwell lived when he was staying in Edinburgh) Mrs. Crockett ran to the door in her nightgown. Just at that moment, eleven men emerged from Blackfriars' Gate. She grabbed one of them by his silk cloak and asked him where the explosion had occurred. He did not answer her. Mrs. Crockett saw the eleven men divide into two parties—four of them went northwards up Blackfriars' Wynd towards the High Street, seven went in the direction of the Cowgate Port, an opening in the Town Wall.

In the days that followed, Mrs. Martin and Mrs. Crockett, respectable Edinburgh housewives, talked freely about the events of that night, as they had good excuse to do. They were, as it chanced, the nearest independent witnesses to a crime which had far-reaching consequences for Scotland, England and the religious struggle in Western Europe: the murder of Henry Stewart, Lord Darnley, known at the time as Henry, King of Scots, through his marriage eighteen months earlier to Mary Stuart.

1 The finest she

On one point contemporary opinion about the Queen of Scotland is unanimous. She was beautiful.

'The finest she that ever was,' said Sir Thomas Randolph, who, as Queen Elizabeth's ambassador in Edinburgh, had no particular reason to gush over a dangerous and unpredictable woman. 'A queen and a paragon,' said the Earl of Lennox, who to his sorrow was Mary's father-in-law. 'La plus belle et la plus cruelle princesse du monde,' said the young Frenchman Chastelard, who, having admired her too much as the first and found her too late to be the second, was on his way to the scaffold. Brantôme insists that even the Scottish language, rural, barbarous and ill-sounding, was 'très belle' on her lips. Ronsard paid her a tribute in his stateliest manner:

> ... 'Ainsi sur toute en beauté nonpareille
> Des Ecossais la Princesse reluit.'

In fact, the death mask, if it is hers, provides all the proof that is needed of Mary's passionate, wilful and extraordinary beauty. Imagination can add the dazzling skin, the grey eyes, the chestnut hair; the brilliant clothes she could draw from her wardrobe at Holyrood which contained sixty gowns and fourteen cloaks, besides basquines, devants, and thirty-three dresses used for masques at Court; the superb jewels which numbered 180 pieces, and included the Great Harry given her by Henri II of France; the presence of a great lady who had been brought up by Diane de Poitiers to shine in the Louvre and Fontainebleau; the pride of a princess who was a direct descendant of Robert Bruce, who was a great-grand-daughter of Henry VII of England, who counted, through her mother and the House of Guise, both Charlemagne and St. Louis among her ancestors. She had been Queen of France, she was Queen of Scotland, she would be, if her plans matured—she would have said, if her rights were recognised—Queen of England.

Vast pretensions, inordinate pride of race, rank, beauty—to these were added a considerable private income. As Queen Dowager of France, Mary enjoyed, to the day of her death, the revenues of the Duchy of Touraine and the county of Poitou. They brought her about twice as much as she drew annually from the Crown revenues of Scotland.

As a Guise, Mary was a member of the most thrusting and greedy clan in France, allied in blood to the semi-German, semi-sovereign house of Lorraine. Three of her uncles had intrigued, cajoled and fought their way to two French duchies and a marquisate. Two others had entered the Church; both were cardinals. The sixth was the Grand Prior of France. Uncle Charles, to whom Mary was particularly attached, was Cardinal of Lorraine and Archbishop of Rheims, enjoying the revenues of eleven French abbeys. When the Pope spoke disapprovingly of pluralism on so spectacular a scale, the Cardinal replied that he would gladly exchange his own benefices for those of His Holiness.

The Guises were magnificent in presence, consummate in charm and energy. They were audacious, vindictive and cursed with a volcanic temper which could explode in acts of abominable cruelty. They were 'the foreigners', against whom the French Princes of the Blood, the Bourbons, and their Protestant supporters raised their voices and pursued their conspiracies.

It was not enough that the Guises should hold a sheaf of the most glittering offices in France: they looked farther and higher, it was thought, to principalities and kingdoms. Charles de Guise, Cardinal of Lorraine, was only half joking when he offered to exchange benefices with the Pope. He had an eye on the Tiara.

Meanwhile they disputed the government of France, under its easy-going, affectionate, weak and bigoted King Henri II, with Anne de Montmorency, the Constable, with Diane de Poitiers, the King's ageing mistress, and with a third influence, at first withdrawn, scarcely perceptible but destined to grow in power and statesmanship, the king's Italian wife, Catherine de' Medici.

Over Mary Stuart, child of a Guise mother and already, by Henri's grace, enjoying precedence at Court over his own

Diane de Poitiers Duchesse de Valentinois

A painting by Clouet

daughters, the family watched with a protective and calculating care. Petted and captivated by them, she was their spy, their eager instrument, a queen they could use as a pawn. When the breath of scandal blew near the child the clan reacted with fiery zeal.

This happened when pretty Lady Fleming, a Scottish widow who had come over to France as Mary's governess, was involved in an amorous scrape. The Guises suspected that behind the affair lurked their political rival the Constable, Montmorency, seeking to besmirch the young Queen through her household. At a hastily summoned family council they decreed that Montmorency must be killed.

However, a closer watch on Lady Fleming revealed not one man near her bedroom but two: King Henri was the widow's lover. Montmorency was acting as decoy for his royal master.

After that the matter was put in the hands of Diane de Poitiers, who played her part with dramatic zest, accusing the King of dishonouring the young Queen by giving her a whore as a governess. Lady Fleming retired from Court and after an easy pregnancy, which she attributed to the royal blood of the child, bore Henri a son.

Mary Stuart resumed her lessons with Diane de Poitiers, who taught her the simple and stately manners of the old French aristocracy, now being corrupted by the Italianate ways which Catherine de' Medici was bringing in. The purpose of the Guises was to make their niece, Mary Stuart, wife of the heir to the throne. This they accomplished in spite of the resourceful opposition of Montmorency when—sole redeeming episode in a ruinous war against Spain and England—the Duc de Guise captured Calais. Mary Tudor died heart-broken; Mary Stuart became wife of the Dauphin. It was a reward conferred on her uncle; the price paid by the French king for Calais.

The money for the wedding festivities was obtained through the ingenuity of the Cardinal of Lorraine, who had a talent for finance. He persuaded the King's bankers to accept a mere quarter of the interest due them on outstanding loans. The nuptials in Notre-Dame lacked nothing in splendour. Nor was it overlooked that the bride had dynastic claims far wider than the bounds of her impoverished little kingdom. Ronsard, in stately verse, congratulated Henri II on having a son who united not only Scotland with France but

England too. Fifteen months later, Henri died, accidentally killed in a tournament by the lance of Gabriel Montgomery, captain of his Scottish Archers. Mary Stuart was Queen of France. Ostentatiously, the Guises escorted her and the new King to the Louvre. This was going to be their reign.

The reign of François II was mercifully short. The Guises found themselves enmeshed in a web of hostile conspiracy, secretly fomented against them among Protestants by the Prince de Condé, second Prince of the Blood. It was intangible, sinister and dangerous as a fog at sea. It was something more than a demonstration and less than a rebellion, more than a Huguenot plot and less than a social revolt.

They responded to their peril, which roused in them an almost superstitious dread, first with febrile energy bordering on panic—the whole Court, Mary Stuart among the others, was shut up in the Château of Amboise, as if taking refuge from a plague—then with fiendish cruelty. The Duc felt a soldier's revulsion from disorder; the Cardinal, his brother, was all the more sadistic because he had flirted intellectually with Protestant ideology.

During the whole of one afternoon fifty-six of the leaders of the agitation were slowly tortured to death in the courtyard of the castle. While the Duc de Guise's Italian wife was driven into a fit of hysterics by the horror, Mary Stuart watched and listened, to the psalms and the screams, with a queenly sangfroid.

Her role in the affairs of France was not that of a neutral or a moderate; she was the active partisan of the man she most admired in the world, her uncle François, the Duc. To the advancement of his power and policies she applied herself with enthusiasm, enslaving the young King with her beauty and charm, and spying on her mother-in-law Catherine de' Medici, who had opened a secret correspondence with the Protestants.

Mary might not accept as infallible all that her uncles decided, but in the end their interests were hers, their blood was hers. She shared their temperament, the meddling with danger, the wild impulse of fear, the collapse into violence, the courage. She gave them her devotion. Through them she became acquainted with the high secrets of policy.

But what was to become of Mary, the lure of the Guises, when the boy King François II died? Catherine de' Medici had the answer ready. Never again would she allow the entrancing girl to come between one of her sons and his mother. Nor would she suffer Mary to marry the King of Spain's son, Don Carlos, as the Cardinal of Lorraine wished. For that would simply have shifted a main lever of Guise power from one slope of the Pyrenees to the other, and Catherine de' Medici, the 'shopkeeper's daughter', was determined that her son, the new King, Charles IX, should rule in France. Until he could, she would. As for Mary Stuart, the sooner she was packed off home to Scotland, the better!

The young woman who arrived at Leith on an autumn day in 1561 was no innocent plunged suddenly into the difficult business of government. She had received a thorough, if premature, education in bloodshed and fanaticism, conspiracy and intrigue. She had listened to tedious discussions in council and had sat with dignity through exhausting ceremonies of state. She was a finished product of the political and courtly schooling of the high Renaissance. She came from a country where unity was kept, with ever-growing difficulty, by ever-growing armies.

She came to another land on a day when, as one keen, sardonic student of the weather recorded, 'the verray face of heaven did manifestlie speak what comfort was brought unto this country with her, to wit, sorrow, dolour, darkness and all impiety'.

2 An idolatrous chapel

ALTHOUGH NOT RICH ON the scale of her Guise uncles, Mary
could afford to make her court at Holyrood a place of colour and
music. The deficit in the Lord Treasurer's accounts might grow
from year to year, but she was a woman of independent means,
able to live as a princess should. Her palace was more French than
Scottish—in the cuisine, the gardens, the servants, the architecture,
the elegance. It was also Catholic. Alone—or all but alone—in
Scotland, Mary with her Catholic servants attended mass in the
Abbey that rose beside her palace. All this was an affront to the
Calvinists in general and a reason for anxiety to their leaders. For
who could be sure that the tender shoots of the new religion,
planted but six or seven years in the town, watered by prayers and
preachings, would be impervious to those diabolical influences?
The mass was bad enough, but the mass allied to the social prestige
of the monarchy, to luxury and laughter, to fiddling, dancing and
beautiful women—no wonder if, with many a holy groan and
fearful thought, the devout in Edinburgh renewed their exhortations against the 'idolatrous chapel' on the outskirts of their town
which their queen frequented.

John Knox, who had the most penetrating mind and the fiercest
tongue among the Protestants, denounced 'the stinking pride of
women' that clustered in the Court. Their perfume was, to his
sensitive nostrils, almost as offensive as the incense in the Chapel
Royal. Their dresses, with so many tassels and such-like vanities,
seemed to him the outward signs of a deep moral corruption. He
would have been surprised had the case been otherwise.

When Mary arrived in Scotland in August, 1561, 'The sun,' he
reported, 'was not seen to shine two days before, nor two days
after. That prewarning gave God unto us! But alas, the most part

were blind.' As for the Queen's morals, he was willing in charity to defer judgment, yet there could hardly be any doubt which way he expected the verdict to go:'We call her not a whore, but she was brought up in the company of the wildest whoremongers.' The luxuries of Holyrood only confirmed the Reformer in his fears.

In this matter, Knox was, however, simply expressing a point of view common among the severer kind of clergy of all Churches. At the same time as he groaned and denounced in Edinburgh, a Franciscan friar was writing in Paris against the seductive wiles of women's fashions: 'Let us consider what are your habiliments—false hair, wigs, curls, plaits, ear-rings, hairnets . . . robes of velvet, satin, damask and taffeta, altogether shameless and deeply cut back and front as well as being cut square even below the armpits!'[1] What pained the friar in Paris on grounds of morality in general was seen by the Calvinists in Edinburgh as a danger particularly directed at their cause.

Their alarm was reasonable.

Catholicism in Scotland had been suppressed by an Act of Parliament which only three peers had opposed. In all history, no revolution is so complete, so decisive or so painless as the suppression of the old Catholic Church in Scotland. It breathed its last in 1560, with no anguish and with hardly a mourner at the deathbed. The reason for this peaceful passing was simple enough, if scarcely creditable to those concerned. A financial settlement was made under which the Catholic clergy kept two-thirds of their rents in the form of annuities during their life; the remaining one-third was divided equally between the Crown and the Calvinist ministers.

By an arrangement so generous to the priests of the defeated Church, the lazy, the tepid and the corrupt were contented, the fiercer Protestants like John Knox lifted up their voices in furious, but impotent, indignation, and Scotland bought a bloodless end to the great feud dividing the Western world. Where there had been a vast, imposing ecclesiastical structure there was suddenly only a heap of rubble on which the dust was settling.

The old Church had no longer a place in the life of Edinburgh, Leith, Dundee, Perth or any of the busy contentious little burghs where the nation's trade, such as it might be, was carried on. In

1. Herbert Norris, *Costume and Fashion*, III, 1938, J. M. Dent and Sons, London.

the countryside, faith followed the feudal chief, and most of the Scottish lords were Protestants.

But, in the victory of Reform, self-interest had played a part along with conviction. Who was to say how strong the new religion would prove should a day of adversity come? There were areas of Scotland where the old fires burned underground, areas where the altars were empty, but the pulpit still was silent, areas where the local magnates' allegiance was doubtful.

The Council of Trent came to an end in the last weeks of 1563; the Counter-Reformation had been launched. The great ordeal of Protestantism in France was at hand. A crisis was approaching in which the personality and intentions of the Queen in Holyrood would be crucial.

Mary Stuart was a young woman of talent and tenacity who made no bones about her religion or her policy. On the eve of her arrival in Scotland, when she was still a girl of nineteen, she gave an audience to the English ambassador in Paris, Sir Nicholas Throckmorton.

'Well, I will be plain with you,' she told him. 'The religion which I profess I take to be the most acceptable to God and, indeed, neither do I know nor desire to know any other. Constancy becometh all folks well, but none better than princes and such as have rule over realms, and especially in matters of religion.

'I have been brought up in this religion, and who would trust me in anything if I should show myself light in this case. For my part, you may perceive that I am none of those who change their religion every year. And, as I told you in the beginning, I mean to constrain none of my subjects, but would wish that they were all as I am; and I trust they will have no support to constrain me.'

These were spirited words, superbly phrased. They did not fail to impress the Englishman with the vehement temperament and dangerous ability of the young woman who uttered them. Even deeper and more painful was the impression made on the champions of the new religion in Scotland.

Mary's words, spoken to Throckmorton and repeated in substance to John Knox, plainly meant that, when she could, she would allow Catholicism the freedom to spread its wings anew in Scotland. Until that day she would hold herself free to practise it, setting what an example, giving what a lead to her subjects!

It was impossible to ignore the menace of Mary's resolve, impossible to put it aside with a tolerant smile as the outburst of a girl not long released from the influence of the nuns of St. Germainen-Laye. John Knox certainly had no doubt that a decisive struggle lay ahead: 'I see the battle shall be great and I am come, I praise my God, even in the brunt of the battle.'

While Mary Stuart lived she did not easily rouse sentimentality among those who met her. The fascination which quickly won devotion, or awoke desire, was, it seems, accompanied by another and colder quality which almost as quickly repelled it. One who turned on her a penetrating and malignant gaze reported that he found 'a proud mind, a crafty wit and an indurate heart'.

Even if this testimony of Mary's most implacable enemy is put aside, the truth remains that in the final judgment of her friends a kind of despair mingled with the admiration. How strange, too, that one of the loveliest and most gifted women of her age was, so far as is known, loved by so few men and, by them, for so short a time!

Had John Knox not feared her so much and hated what he feared, he might have detected that Mary had courage as well as cunning, and that both these qualities were strangely interwoven with a self-dramatising and excitable nature, bordering on hysteria.

In all her life there is one recorded moment of supreme enjoyment, when she took the field with her half-brother James and broke the power of the Earl of Huntly in pitched battle. It was an unimportant little campaign, although it yielded Mary a sizable booty, and her brother the earldom of Moray. But it gave her something more—the exhilaration of danger, the throb of intense physical exertion, the cruel pleasure of war.

'I never saw her merrier, never dismayed,' reported an Englishman who was there. 'She was sorry for only one thing—that she was not a man to know what life it was to lie all night in the fields or to walk the street with a buffcoat and a steel cap, a Glasgow buckler and a broadsword.'

This fierce side of Mary was genuine and natural enough. Was she not the niece of the most brilliant and bloodthirsty soldiers in France? It was not, however, the only aspect of her character.

The fiery temper could break under strain and the flow of lucid words would turn suddenly into a flood of tears. She had with a woman's emotional weakness the temperament of a man of action;

what she needed were the gifts of the statesman: patience, caution, dissimulation. Her motto should have been that of her mother-in-law, Catherine de' Medici—'Hate and wait'.

Since she came to Scotland, Mary had been asked to do too much and to do it alone. The task set her by the grand strategy of Catholic resurgence in Europe was once, twice, three times impossible. Consider what she was and what was asked of her.

She was the Catholic sovereign of a country in which Protestant-ism, in its most logical and belligerent form, had gained an ascendancy. Given the fanatical mood of the age, such an incompatibility between queen and subjects could not persist for long. Besides, it was her purpose, unalterable and undisguised, to change the religion of Scotland as opportunity served, and to create the opportunity if she could do so. Even if the Protestant leaders in Scotland had been blind or craven—and they were neither the one nor the other—they were even less likely to rest peaceably under an active Catholic monarch than under a passive one.

Finally, as the great-grand-daughter of Henry VII, Mary was the nearest heiress and successor of Queen Elizabeth. Indeed, all Catholic Europe thought that she was already the rightful Queen of England—successor of Mary Tudor—and Mary Stuart herself shared that conviction. While she was Queen of France, she and her boy husband had used the royal arms of England and had conferred favours as Queen and King of England.

By the Treaty of Edinburgh, made at a time—1560—when an English fleet was in the Firth of Forth, an English army was under the ramparts of Leith, and a French army manned those ramparts, a Scottish Government had agreed that Mary would no longer use the Arms of England; Elizabeth's title as Queen of her own land was to be recognised. Mary, at that time still in France, refused to ratify the treaty. She never did ratify it.

Holyrood was, for her, only a brief halting-place between the Louvre, where she had glittered as Dauphine and reigned for a few months as Queen, and Whitehall, temporarily usurped by her cousin.

When she looked out from Holyrood, southward over the gardens, over the park with its deer and conies to Arthur's Seat, she never forgot that beyond lay England, ruled by Anne Boleyn's daughter. By birth and conviction, Mary was committed to a rivalry holding deadly danger to herself and Elizabeth alike. Neither of these princesses was unaware of the nature of the war between them, or of the likely fate of the vanquished. 'Strike or be stricken. Strike or be stricken,' whispered Elizabeth Tudor to herself when, years later, she was screwing up her will to kill Mary Stuart.

The prizes were dazzling; the knives were sharp; the arena in which the conflict was fought out was a kingdom, half tribal, half feudal and wholly anarchic, more Celtic than Angle, with a strong infusion of Norse, in which a feeble monarchy strove, with varying success, to hold at bay a pack of gilded ruffians, the Scottish nobility.

Lest the phrase be thought too harsh, a few examples may usefully be adduced. Gilbert Kennedy, Earl of Cassillis, was about twenty-six years of age in 1567. He had, a few months before, changed his religion from Catholic to Protestant on marrying a daughter of Lord Glamis who brought him a respectable dowry.

The young Kennedy was not content, however, to depend on marriage in order to further his fortunes. He had, in particular, a fancy for the lands of Glenluce in Galloway belonging to the abbey of Crossraguel. With a monk as his accomplice, he forged the signature of the former abbot to a lease of the property. After that he hired 'a carle called Carnochan' to murder the monk, prevailed on his uncle the Laird of Bargany to hang the carle, and so acquired the lands.

It does not appear that the Earl was troubled in conscience over such a deplorable sequence of events, in which respect he differed from Matthew Stewart, Earl of Lennox. This important nobleman had taken the English side twenty years earlier when Scotland was laid waste by the Duke of Somerset's army. Lennox forced some Scotsmen to fight in his ranks by holding their sons as hostage. When the fathers deserted, the children were hanged. It was believed that, from then onwards, the Earl of Lennox had a superstitious terror of being left alone, 'a disease', as his wife said, 'which solitariness is most against'.

Archibald Campbell, Earl of Argyll, had no such deed of blood on his soul, but those who knew him best trusted him least. Between him and his wife Jean, a half-sister of the Queen, a bitter dislike reigned. She was afraid to join the Earl in his castle at Inveraray lest, as she put it, she came to 'a hard end'.

Such were the men who, with the sanction of dungeon and gallows, ruled their provinces like sovereigns, conceding to the central power only as much deference as was necessary and politically convenient. They were united, family with family, in an infinitely complicated criss-crossing of relationships. They were divided by hatreds, some as old as time itself, some as fresh as a recent and ill-starred rebellion ending in the forfeiture of land by one and the grant of land to another. They were, as their fathers had been before them, touchy and vengeful, stupid and sly, brave and shifty, capable of a strong Scottish feeling which could in a flash—on some slight to their lordships' honour—turn towards treason, especially if the Queen of England's paymaster was there to chink her gold pieces!

Beneath them in the social scale were the lairds. Holding their lands directly from the Crown but lacking the lustre of nobility, they were of the same stamp as the peers, of lesser scope but equal cupidity. Further down still were the burgesses, beginning after all these centuries to think and, more dangerous still, to speak. And the peasants, keeping their heads down, going about their business, leaving their masters to rule, and mis-rule.

Into the shifting but inveterate patterns of family feuds and clan vendettas the religious schism had injected its fresh complexities in Scotland, as elsewhere in Europe.

The Abbot Mina, an intimate friend of Mary's uncle, the Cardinal of Lorraine, wrote one day to a man who supplied news to the Spanish ambassador in Paris:

'In the past, friends and foes were distinguished by the boundaries of provinces and kingdoms; men were called English, German, French, Spaniards, Italians. Today one should only speak of Catholics or heretics. A Catholic prince should reckon as friends all the Catholics of all lands, just as heretics consider all heretics as their friends and subjects.'

This novel view, confusing the old loyalties and animosities in Europe, could not leave Mary's kingdom untouched.

But the ancient Scotland faded more slowly than the new emerged. Feudal loyalties survived, able still to exert their power over men caught up in the venomous theological debate. Although

John Knox had reason to distrust the Earl of Bothwell as a Protestant friend of the Catholic Queen, he was conscious of older ties between them. 'My lord,' he said one day, 'my great-grandfather, good sir, and father have served your lordship's predecessors, and some of them have died under their standards.'

The old Celtic Scotland lived on beside the feudal, and remembered its cherished quarrels in the ideological era. The Earl of Argyll, the most influential chieftain of the Western Highlands, kept an eye on the twists and turns of intrigue in Edinburgh, without allowing his mind to be diverted from diplomacy and war in the Islands and in the glens of Antrim.

In these regions lay the traditional and profitable business of his family, to the annoyance of Queen Elizabeth who saw her Irish rebels comforted with Scotch whisky and Gaelic encouragement.

Elizabeth had, however, no moral right to complain: half the nobility of Scotland had taken her money. Prices did not run high: £500 for a regent; £200 or even £100 for an earl or a baron.

Having re-appropriated to their own use much of the estates their ancestors had improvidently given to the Church, the Scottish peerage had acquired a taste for possessions which was not readily appeased. Catholic and Protestant alike, they vied with one another in the pious duty of relieving the clergy of wealth which, it was widely acknowledged, had become a source of spiritual corruption.

Although the country was entering on a period of rapid commercial evolution, marked by acute inflation,[1] there were few visible changes from the Scotland of a generation earlier. The economy was simple and rural. It could feed the half-million people who dwelt in it, apart from the customary intervals of famine when crops failed and cattle died. On the whole, people ate well, were clothed roughly and were housed miserably.

The taste of the gentry followed France. After all, since 1558, every Scotsman had been a naturalised Frenchman and many of the richer among them had finished their education in Paris.

Trade—the wine business with Bordeaux apart—was with the Low Countries and Scandinavia. Scottish ships took abroad fish, fine skins, inferior cloth and salt; they brought home timber and finery. For sophisticated crafts did not exist and native forests were

1. A sixfold rise in the cost of wine between 1550 and 1625.

few. In some favoured areas the soil was excellent for grain; elsewhere it raised sheep and cattle. Hunting was good; wolves were a nuisance—sometimes a danger.

The burghs furnished one-sixth of the nation's taxes and clung savagely to their monopoly of foreign trade. In them, in their literate, articulate, Protestant populations and in the watchful, censorious pastors, were the seeds of the Scotland that was to be. In the meantime, they upheld the dignity of the merchant caste against those who practised manual skills, or who dressed like peasants or allowed their wives to be seen in the streets wearing an apron.

By far the chief among the burghs was the capital city, Edinburgh. It was in plan rather like the skeleton of a fish, stretched west to east on a ridge sloping down from the Castle to Holyrood. The spine of the fish was the High Street, the ribs were certain narrow and noisome alleys. About halfway from castle to palace, the town proper ended and, with no interruption in the buildings, the Canongate began, a village largely dependent on the Court. At this point the street was spanned by the Netherbow, one of the eight gates piercing the Town Wall which had encircled Edinburgh ever since the disastrous Scottish defeat at Flodden half a century earlier.

Edinburgh was a crowded little town of, perhaps, as many as 10,000 inhabitants. Big enough to have the courts of justice, the Exchequer, a royal castle, a royal palace, and the town houses of the nobles; small enough to ensure that any remarkable local event was swiftly known in every quarter. With John Knox and his lieutenant John Craig as its ministers, the town was in the very forefront of Calvinist orthodoxy, even if it could not be assumed that God's saints were utterly impervious to fleshly temptations.

In the Canongate parish, the Rev. John Brand, his fourteen elders and eight deacons, were painfully aware that they held an outpost against the hosts of Satan entrenched in the Queen's chapel. In the Canongate the collision between country and court, Calvin and Rome, virtue and vice, was most dramatically apparent. The statistics of the parish have something to say—1200 at communion in 1566; but, alas, of the 137 children baptised in the year by John Brand, eleven were bastards; and fifty-seven women living in the parish were named as common harlots. It seems, all things considered, a figure on the high side. But the explanation is surely not far to seek.

The dangerous proximity of aliens and courtiers has left its deep, deplorable traces on the Kirk Sessions records: Katherine Lenton, thrice called, accused and now convicted by her own confession for harlotry with the French ambassador was 'decreed to be branked,[1] her head cropped on one side and clipped on the other, to be set upon the cross and there to remain the space of three hours'. More heinous still was the offence of Paul Wallis who married a woman at mass in the Queen's chapel. Wallis was handed over to the civil magistrate and by him was sentenced to eight days in gaol. For the lay and ecclesiastical authorities could in no way approve such marriages, 'nor in any way authorise anything that is done in that idolatrous chapel contrary to God and His word'.

The earnest, vigilant community of the Canongate Kirk in which each member was for ever searching the conduct of the others for signs of backsliding and error and the Court, luxurious (as the time went), frivolous and Catholic—only a few yards divided them, yet what prospect was there that they would ever live in peace together? How could Mary Stuart remain Queen of Scots when John Brand and his like believed that her works were suspect and her faith was heathen? Even if there had been no embroilments from abroad, no tampering with loyalties, no ambitions and cupidities to be excited to bloody deeds, the situation in Edinburgh would have been desperate enough. But the town was a nest of snakes.

English spies, English traitors, England's creatures—in the closes and wynds one brushed against them constantly, as they eavesdropped, whispered and changed sides. There were men like Kirkcaldy of Grange, a fine soldier, proved in the French wars, a traitor in the pay of Elizabeth's secret service and, in the end, a martyr in Mary Stuart's cause. Or Christopher Rokesby, reputed to be so devout that he heard mass three times a day. He had fled from England, pursued by a writ of execution for £1000, and had two private audiences with Mary in Edinburgh Castle, she sitting on a little coffer without a cushion, he kneeling beside her. The Queen with seeming artlessness told him of her plans to stir up a Papist rising in England.

1. i.e. put in a bridle kept for scolds, witches, etc.

In the meantime, Rokesby had been in touch with the authorities in his own country as 'a poor gentleman of England in some adversity. Please use me with secrecy.' Promised money and pardon, he wrote for Sir William Cecil's eye all that Mary had told him. But, alas for Rokesby, the ears of Scottish espionage in London had picked up the hint that he was not to be trusted. His room in Edinburgh was searched. Cecil heard the bad news: 'Rokesby is taken, with all his papers; among them, I fear, your letter.' The poor gentleman of England spent the next twenty-one months in a disagreeable dungeon in Spynie Castle.

One after another, the underpinnings of social order were giving way beneath the strains of the political and religious revolution. 'It is a pity,' mourned the English ambassador, 'to hear the lamentation among all sorts of men, the Papists that mislike her [Mary's] manners and the Protestants that know the likelihood of God's word to be overthrown. . . . The Borders never in worse order, more murder and spoil among them. Within these six days a discord risen between Lord Yester and the Homes; Lord Seton looked for, who hath quarrel with the Douglas, the Earl Bothwell, enemy to all honest men, written for; Edinburgh never so without order.'

In such conditions, it was easy enough for such as Rokesby to find their way to Edinburgh. The Queen's writ did not run southwards of the city farther than a morning's ride. Then began the belt of unkempt moorland called the Border, stretching over the greater part of five Scottish and two English counties. There, allegiance was dubious, war, private or national, was the pastime of the people, and the law no better than a rare intruder, as brutal as the times and the men required.

By bridle paths known only to the local moss troopers, a busy two-way traffic in letters, spies, traitors and fugitives from justice went on between Scotland and the powerful, uneasy neighbour to the south. Ships took salt from Scotland to London and brought letters back. Agents, in disguise, came ashore at Leith from the Continent. In this way the Pope's nuncio had brought Mary an invitation to send her representative to the Council of Trent. A watchful Englishman caught sight of the prelate, scurrying down a corridor in Holyrood while Mary's Protestant courtiers were at the sermon.

The young Queen, half a foreigner to her people in upbringing and religion, altogether a foreigner to them in the aim and reach of her policy, faced an agonising complex of problems. She must maintain the precarious hold of the monarchy in Scotland, a country in which national vanity was high and civil morality was debased. She was expected to promote and, at some chosen moment, to achieve a dynastic coup in a neighbouring kingdom, vastly richer than her own, more powerful, brilliantly ruled and swelling with national self-confidence.

All this was preparing in the midst of a religious revolution in which, already, every horror was permitted and every fear was justified. In the opinion of intelligent men everywhere, the worst abominations of the Christian civil war, tortures, murders, massacres, still lay ahead. The atmosphere all over Europe verged on frenzy. Every step that Mary took, however stealthy and faltering, awakened enormous echoes of alarm or hope. She was, at once, the most dangerous woman in Europe and the most helpless.

On what and on whom could she count, this widow in her early twenties? On her Scottish and French revenues eked out by irregular funds sent her by Spain or the Pope. On the artillery and ammunition in her fortresses of Dunbar, Edinburgh, Stirling and Dumbarton. On 200 arquebusiers hired to guard her person and palace.

On whose counsel could she lean? On her Guise uncle, the Cardinal of Lorraine, who was fond of her? It was even whispered —a typical invention—that at one time the Cardinal had been her incestuous lover. But this was only one of the earliest of the slanders that pursued her through life. Ironically, it was spread by Lord Bothwell, the central figure in a later and better-attested scandal. Certainly it may be conceded that nothing in His Eminence's character makes the slander impossible.

As an adviser to the young Queen of Scotland, the Cardinal was defective in important respects: he was too far off, in Rheims or Paris, and he knew little or nothing about Scottish affairs.

Mary might turn—and for a time did turn—to her half-brother James, whom she had made Earl of Moray. He behaved in a friendly, brotherly fashion to her and then—for what reason?— forsook her. He was a Calvinist, sincere and strict: capable, brave and, above all, ambitious. But he was a pensioner of England's, Mary could not trust him and could not share some of the secrets of her policy with him. In the end, she pursued him with implacable hatred.

Then there was William Maitland of Lethington, her Secretary of State. This laird from Lauderdale, who had received at the Court of Henri II an education almost as profoundly French as that of Mary herself, was one of the subtlest, most tortuous diplomats of the age. If only the age had been less fanatical, less concerned with men's ultimate convictions, more willing to enjoy the dance of high intrigue for its own intricate sake, this able, smooth and witty Scotsman might have shone more brightly and come to a better end. But Maitland, who put politics above religion, was bound to appear an atheist to Catholics and Calvinists alike.

At one time when it was thought that Mary might marry the French King Charles IX, Maitland, who had spent some time in France with the Cardinal of Lorraine, was suspected of being involved in the affair. Cecil wrote to him in alarm at this prospect of a new Catholic marriage. His tone was solemn: in matters like this, 'no wisdom of the world, no affection to persons, no care of ourselves ought to blind us'. He continued: 'My Lord, I require in God's name, before whom you and I will stand without advocate, let no respect move you to allow of that which is intended to set up Antichrist' (i.e. the Pope). 'I mean much therein and, if you will not understand it, I think all the rest of my writing little worth.'

On Lethington the gravity of this rebuke was lost, yet it was the gravity of the age he lived in. Nor was he any more likely to hold the confidence of Mary's Catholic advisers than that of Cecil. For Lethington, like Moray, was taking Elizabeth's money.

It was not all gaiety and music in the little château under the crags of Arthur's Seat. Passing the lounging guards, crossing the drawbridge, moving along the panelled corridors and the state-rooms hung with fine French tapestries of the Labours of Hercules and—Mary's favourite—the victory at Ravenna under Gaston de Foix, or the portraits of Scottish kings and Mary's relatives, Valois or Guise; reaching the inner rooms where the Queen's wardrobe was stored, where her jewels, diamonds and rubies, the Great Harry itself, the six strings of black pearls 'like black muscades' she had been given by that swarthy, despised Italian, Catherine de' Medici, were locked in their coffers, came Anxiety, the chilly visitor, the silencer of music. Like Elizabeth, far more truly than Elizabeth, Mary was alone. Like Elizabeth, she was in deadly danger. Soon the danger grew.

In the space of a few months, from December 1564, Mary made three important decisions. She appointed David Riccio her French secretary. She restored James Hepburn, Earl of Bothwell, to his former post as Lieutenant of the Border. And she married Henry, Lord Darnley. Each decision was calamitous.

3   A bass for the quartet

DAVID RICCIO, BORN AT Pancalieri near Turin about 1533, had taken service first with the Archbishop of Turin and then, at Nice, in the court of the Duke of Savoy. He arrived in Edinburgh, in the autumn of 1561, as a valet in the suite of Robertino Solaro di Moretta, the Duke's ambassador to the Queen of Scotland. As he had a good bass voice and as Mary wanted one to complete her quartet of singers, she took him into her household. At the end of 1564 he became Mary's French secretary, although, in fact, he wrote French with some difficulty. But he was 'a merry fellow and a good musician' and, as an Italian and a good son of the Church, he was likely to be reliable.

Soon Riccio was in charge of all the Queen's secret correspondence, Secretary of State in fact if not in name. Soon he was known to have the Queen's ear, and soon, as a natural result, he was well-off, able to buy jewels for the Queen, able to buy horses, velvet hose, satin doublets, armour, pistols and swords[1] for himself.

Before long, reports and rumours were flying about Edinburgh and thence to London. Riccio, they whispered, was an ugly, black-jowled foreigner, in all likelihood an agent of the Pope's. There is no evidence that he was anything of the sort, but it is obviously not impossible. Certainly it seems curious that he and his brother Joseph should arrive in Edinburgh, as they did, in the suites of two different ambassadors.

As a domestic, advanced far beyond his station, Riccio displayed the lack of breeding that was to be expected. He bore himself altogether too much as if he were the equal of nobles and gentlemen. There was indeed a story, almost incredible in its enormity, that the Queen, in her infatuation, meant to make the upstart a peer and

1. He had twenty-two at the time of his death.

chancellor of the realm! More plausibly, it was said that Mary contemplated hiring a bodyguard of Italians.

This project caused great annoyance among the Protestant party. It was a clear indication, they said, that Mary meant to tyrannise over the country. 'How grievous it was,' grumbled those noblemen, hardened in every kind of treason, 'that a sovereign should mistrust her own subjects, and commit her person to the guard of strangers and Papists!' Besides, Riccio, as an Italian himself, would make his fellow-countrymen do what he pleased!

Passing from criticism to slander, the rumour-mongers of Edinburgh alleged that Mary liked Riccio's company altogether too much, was altogether too free with the Italian singer. In short, many professed to believe that David Riccio had become Mary Stuart's lover.

Long years afterwards, Mary committed to writing her opinions about the place of the nobility in society. They might be great, she argued, but this greatness must not impinge on the rights of the sovereign. The sovereign's authority came from God, that of the nobles from the sovereign under God. She went on, in an obvious reference to Riccio: 'If the King finds a man of low estate, poor in goods but generous in spirit, faithful in heart and fit for the task required of him, he will commit authority to that man, risking the dislike of the magnates.'

Between a God-endowed monarch and a king-chosen nobility the difference was obviously more than one of degree. The doctrine of the gulf between the Lord's anointed and the aristocracy might be respectable enough in philosophical terms, but it was not likely to be a good guide to policy in the Scotland of the 1560's.

In any country the role of favourite carries with it a certain degree of risk. When the favourite is foreign, and the country is Scotland, the risks are acute. Sir James Melville, who was perhaps the most sensible and level-headed of Mary's diplomats, warned both the Queen and Riccio of the dangers they were running, but Mary would not, and Riccio could not, heed the advice he gave them.

The case of the Earl of Bothwell was another matter altogether. This swaggering, quarrelsome young nobleman was the hereditary Lord High Admiral of Scotland and the owner of big estates in

Lothian and the Borders. He was unpopular with his peers and better liked by the commoners. One incident in his past was remembered. With some followers he had waylaid an English subsidy on its way to Scottish rebels. Sir William Cecil's emissary had been relieved of 3157 crowns (say £1000 sterling) after a sharp skirmish on a dark night. The 'unhonourable and thievish act' was as likely to give satisfaction in Scotland as to displease Queen Elizabeth.

In political affairs Bothwell took a solitary path. He was loyal both to the Queen and to the Protestant religion. In speech he was coarse and in appearance uncouth, but, like many men of his kind, he had a way with women accompanied by a marked sexual appetite. As time went on and his enemies grew in numbers and virulence, his reputation gathered the customary reproaches. Bothwell was charged with heresy—reasonably enough, in the eyes of the Vatican—witchcraft and sodomy.

Until the autumn of 1565 Bothwell was living abroad, banished by the Queen. This period of exile followed an outbreak of high spirits into which he lured the Queen's youngest uncle, René, Marquis d'Elbœuf, and her half-brother, Lord John Stewart.

Bothwell had discovered that Lord Arran, heir of the first nobleman in Scotland, the Duke of Chatelherault, was in the habit of visiting a handsome, obliging wench, an Edinburgh merchant's daughter named Alison Craig. Taking a broad-minded view of these goings-on, Alison's father-in-law allowed the lovers to meet in his house in St. Mary's Wynd. There, one night just before Christmas, 1561, Bothwell with his two companions hoped to surprise Arran and his light o' love. They were disappointed. Arran had been tipped off in time.

Edinburgh, that rowdy little capital, resounded with the scandal. The Kirk, which looked on Arran as one of its own chosen vessels, declared that the horror of the facts 'commoved all godly hearts'. The powerful Hamilton clan, of which Arran's father was head, felt itself to be affronted. Three hundred armed and indignant Hamiltons gathered in the town, resolved to set upon Bothwell and his companions as they returned from a Christmas Eve dinner. But this design was a secret Edinburgh was too small to keep.

Hearing the news, Bothwell, d'Elbœuf and Lord John collected a force of their own, bigger than that of the Hamiltons. A murderous affray was about to break out in the streets. The joke had gone too far.

Palace and town were warned. At nine o'clock the tocsin rang; pike-trailing burgesses poured into the streets ready to defend the peace; and from Holyroodhouse came the Queen's brother Lord James Stewart and Lord Huntly with threats that restored order within half an hour. Next day Bothwell and Arran were summoned to appear before the Queen.

The sequel to the fracas was that Bothwell and Arran made up their quarrel. Then Arran went mad and accused his father the Duke of conspiring with Bothwell to kidnap the Queen and lock her in Dumbarton Castle. Those who wished to believe the story did so. One of them was Lord James Stewart, who prevailed on his sister the Queen to imprison Bothwell in Edinburgh Castle. But either the gaol was not secure enough or the gaolers not too vigilant.

One August night in 1562, Bothwell escaped and, with no excess of haste, made for France, where he was confident of a welcome from the Guise family. However, a North Sea gale intervened. Stormbound on English soil, Bothwell was captured and thrown into the Tower of London. Permitted at last to cross to France, he applied for the command of that *corps d'élite* in the French service, the Scottish Archers of the Guard. His stay in Paris was full of incident. Suborned by the Scottish Secretary of State, Maitland of Lethington, his servants made an abortive attempt to poison him.

Bothwell received his captaincy in the Archers almost simultaneously with the news that his queen was willing to see him in Scotland again. In March, 1565, the adventurer was reported in Edinburgh, and reinstated as Lieutenant of the Border. This was, for obvious reasons, the key military command in the country, and by giving it to Bothwell, Mary showed that she had given him her trust as well as her forgiveness. Very soon she carried her interest one stage further. She found a wife for Bothwell—Lady Anne Gordon, sister of Lord Huntly. She had already found a husband for herself.

On the face of it, Mary's choice was not wholly maladroit. Henry Stewart, Lord Darnley, was her cousin, with a claim to the English succession only a shade less good than her own. Many Englishmen might indeed have preferred Darnley's as that of one born in the country. He was a tall, slender youth, nineteen years old, whose round, smooth face wore a vacuous, discontented expression. Mary, who had resolved to marry him before she set eyes on him, was not put off by his appearance. After all, she had no great wealth of suitors to choose from. The Cardinal of Lorraine pressed the advantages of a union with the Archduke Karl; Philip II of Spain proposed that she should marry his son, Don Carlos. But it was impossible for her to marry a French, a Spanish or even a German prince without precipitating a quarrel, perhaps a war, with England. And the best Elizabeth could offer Mary from among her subjects was the Earl of Leicester, her own devoted lover. With Robert Dudley, the widower of Amy Robsart, established in Holyrood, the Queen of England would have slept more soundly in her bed. But the Queen of Scotland had no intention of marrying so as to ensure more peaceful nights in Westminster. One of the reasons Mary Stuart lost no time in uniting herself in wedlock with Lord Darnley was that Elizabeth was known to dislike the union. In any case, it was high time Mary was married.

Marriage might be difficult to bring about, as it was in the case of any sovereign princess; it brought perils of its own. But at least, in Mary's case, there operated no hidden physical or psychological veto such as impeded marriage for Elizabeth and saved her for virginity and greatness. Mary was a hot-blooded, hot-tempered young woman of twenty-two, lonely and sorely tried. She needed a man by her side; she wished to have a husband in her bed. Without thinking too long or looking too narrowly, she heaped horses, jewels, clothes and titles on Darnley and made public her resolve to marry him.

The affair was carried through with some haste. Mary sent a messenger to Rome to ask Pope Pius IV for money and a dispensation to marry Darnley. This latter she needed because she and Darnley were in the second degree of consanguinity from one common stem and in the fourth degree from another. In a consistory held in St. Mark's, Rome, on September 1, 1565, the Pope said that it appeared to him that 'there was no reason why he should not immediately grant a dispensation especially as it was to be feared that, if their request were refused, they might hold to their purpose. If they set at naught the authority of the Apostolic

THES BE THE SONES OF Ꝑ RIGHT HONERABLES ꝰERLLE OF LENOXE AD
TE LADY MARGARETꝫ GRACE COVNTYES OF LENOXE AD ANGWYSE

1563

CHARLLES STEWARDE
HIS BROTHER. ÆTATIS. 6.

HENRY STEWARDE LORD DAR̄
LEY AND DOWGLAS. ÆTATIS. 17.

Henry, Lord Darnley, husband of Mary Stuart, with his brother Charles

Reproduced by gracious permission of Her Majesty The Queen

See in this matter, they might do so the same in other things.'

The fears of His Holiness were not unjustified. More than a month before the consistory in St. Mark's, Mary, wearing the widow's weeds of a Queen-Dowager of France, had already married Darnley by the rites of the Catholic Church in the Chapel Royal at Holyrood (July 29, 1565). She heard the nuptial mass; the bridegroom, although a Catholic by repute, did not.

The marriage was not universally approved. Mary's Protestant half-brother, the Earl of Moray, rose in rebellion and mustered an army. John Knox preached a sermon in Edinburgh in which he argued that God had set boys and women in government to punish the sins of the poeple. Darnley, who was in Knox's congregation that day, was so irritated by what he heard that he could not eat his dinner. But, in spite of Knox's exhortations, the bulk of the Protestants in Scotland refused to follow Moray. Without much difficulty, Mary drove him over the Border into England, where Elizabeth (who had subsidised his rebellion) gave him a public scolding.

The papal dispensation was granted with 'paternal affection' on September 24 and arrived in Edinburgh six weeks later. Before the end of the year a new and more militant Pope, Pius V, ruled in the Vatican. He sent Mary his congratulations on her victory over her Protestant half-brother. 'Truly, dearest daughter, you understand the duties of devout kings and queens, the way to establish your rule and consolidate your kingdom.' However, on the matter of money . . . 'The Lord had promised rewards for good holy works, not when begun but when ended—therefore complete what you have commenced, weeding out completely the thorns and tares of heretical depravity. . . .'

By that time, two facts had become manifest: Mary was to have a child. And her marriage was going badly. Darnley, king by title, wanted to be king at law as well so that, if anything should happen to his wife, he would be her successor . . . King of Scots, nearest claimant to the throne of England—the prospect was dazzling enough to fire the imagination and cupidity of any ambitious youth, however level-headed. Darnley was ambitious; he was not notably strong in the head.

Mary felt herself threatened at a point where she would never yield an inch: her sovereign rights. Coins had been minted on which 'Henricus' came before 'Maria'. They were succeeded by a new series in which the order of names was reversed. Darnley sulked and absented himself more and more from Court. He took to the bottle and to the low resorts that abounded in Edinburgh. As the husband's insolence grew more scandalous, the wife's anger gathered force. Mary had a stamp made, so that Darnley's signature could be printed on state documents. Riccio kept the stamp.

Sir Thomas Randolph, Elizabeth's ambassador in Edinburgh, had worked assiduously to bring about a marriage between Mary and the Earl of Leicester. Now he reported that the union with Darnley had produced a dreadful deterioration in the Scottish Queen's character. 'A more wilful woman and one more wedded to her own opinion, without order, reason or discretion, I never did know or hear of. She is so much changed in her nature that she bears only the shape of the woman she was before.' Writing to Leicester, Randolph tactfully attributed this moral decay to Mary's disappointment over being denied so glamorous a consort as the Earl would have been.

The domestic quarrel at Holyrood was an open invitation to every mischief-maker to exacerbate it and turn it to advantage: the Protestants who distrusted Riccio and the nobles who hated him. The preachers, who spoke of Mary as one synonymous with the harlot Jezebel. The exiled Scottish rebels, who kicked their heels in Newcastle or London and dreamed of return and revenge. Maitland of Lethington, who saw his office as Secretary of State filled by a low-born Italian. And Moray who believed—who knew—that he was better fitted than his sister by ability, temperament and religion, to rule the land of which, but for his father's unhappy omission of one formality, he would be King.

Darnley, a bitterly resentful young man with an exaggerated view of his own importance, was easily worked on to become a violently jealous husband as well. His wife treated him like a servant; her advisers regarded him as a schoolboy. If he ever forgot the slight, someone was at hand to remind him of it. 'It is contrary to nature,' Lord Morton told him, 'that the hen should crow before the cock.' Darnley already believed that Riccio's influence was a factor in keeping the crown from him. Soon he was listening to hints that Riccio was his wife's lover, that the child she was carrying would have an Italian father.

Was there anything in these rumours? All that can be said is that Mary was a woman of an age and a class in which manners were notably free. Had she not been brought up by Diane de Poitiers, Duchesse de Valentinois, mistress of one French king and perhaps of two? On the other hand, it was an era in which the blood royal was regarded with peculiar reverence—above all, by princesses.

In March 1566 Darnley signed two secret agreements with the Protestant nobles. Their crimes, whether committed or contemplated, were to be forgiven and their lands restored; he was to receive the Crown Matrimonial, and with it the kingship should his wife die or be deposed for heresy or some other cause. There was something else. 'David, with the consent of the King,' Randolph told Leicester, 'shall have his throat cut within these ten days. Many things more grievous and worse than these are brought to my ears.'

Riccio was to be murdered.

4 *'For life, for life, for life!'*

The *coup d'état* HAD a swift and, as it seemed, a complete success.

About eight o'clock on the night of Saturday, March 9, 1566, the Palace of Holyroodhouse was seized by an armed mob whose task was made easier for them by the fact that Stewart of Traquair, captain of the Queen's Guard, apparently knew what was afoot and kept himself and his men out of the way. The chief strength of the invading party was provided by the Douglas family and its dependents.

At its head was James Douglas, Earl of Morton, a blond, squat, spade-bearded man whose life unpleasantly combined avarice, adultery and piety. With him, ready for the most abominable crime, went his relative, Archibald Douglas, who was a parson at least to the extent of drawing the revenues of the parish of Dundee, and an extraordinary judge of the Court of Session.

An even more sinister figure among the intruders that March evening was Lord Ruthven, clad all in black armour. He was a fanatical Calvinist who, like so many other notable persons of the time, was suspected of witchcraft. He had risen from a sick-bed to carry out an important public duty. The Earl of Lindsay was another of the conspirators.

They overpowered the porter at the main gate, snatched his keys and locked the doors behind them. Once inside the palace, they were met by Darnley, who led eighteen of them, with swords and daggers drawn and pistols cocked, through his apartments to the Queen's presence chamber. There Mary sat at supper with the Countess of Argyll and Lord Robert Stewart (her half-sister and half-brother). The fourth person at the table was David Riccio, wearing a fur-trimmed dressing gown.

Darnley was the first of the conspirators to enter the room. He had spent the afternoon playing tennis with the Italian. Now he put his arm affectionately round the Queen's waist. A moment later Ruthven entered, pale and wasted with illness.

'May it please your majesty,' he said, 'that yonder man Davie come out of your privy chamber where he has been too long.'

'What offence has he committed?' asked the Queen.

'He has offended your honour.'

Putting herself between Riccio and Ruthven, Mary told the noblemen to leave.

A moment later armed men poured into the room. The table was overturned. The candles crashed to the floor, all but one, which Lady Argyll caught. Riccio, clinging to the Queen's dress, was brutally prised free by a Border laird named Andrew Ker of Fawdonside and dragged screaming from the room. The murderers, making sure of their purpose, stabbed him fifty-six times before they desisted. Darnley's dagger was left conspicuously in the body, although whether he planted it there or not is uncertain.

When the butchery was over, Ruthven returned to the Queen's chamber and sat down. Different accounts are given of the scene that followed, although on essentials they agree. Ugly, common-place and melodramatic, its like has been narrated in countless divorce courts.

Darnley charged the Queen with denying him his rights as a husband. Night after night she had sat up playing cards with Riccio until two or three in the morning. That was all the entertainment he, her husband, had enjoyed with her for months.

'It is not the wife's part to go to the husband,' Mary retorted.

'When I came to your room,' said Darnley, 'either you refused or you said you were ill.'

'Well, you have taken your last of me.'

At this point Ruthven put his word in: 'That would be a pity. He is your majesty's husband. You must do your duty to each other.'

Mary turned on him.

'Why may I not leave him as your wife left *her* husband?' she asked, and broke down in passionate tears.

Ruthven, feeling faint, asked for a drink. Wine was brought him by a French servant of the household.

Meanwhile, in his quarters in the palace, Lord Bothwell was

entertaining Lords Huntly and Atholl to supper. When they heard the war-cry 'A Douglas, A Douglas!' they knew that some mischief was afoot. With servants, cooks and anyone else whom they could muster, they made for the sounds of disturbance, but their way was barred by a door held against them by Douglas retainers. Bothwell returned to his rooms where, in due course, Ruthven came to tell him what had happened. The plot, he said, was aimed only at Riccio, who was now dead.

Far from reassured by this information, Bothwell and Huntly sought a way out of the Palace. At last they came on a window looking out on the little garden where from time immemorial the royal lions, the heraldic beasts of Scotland, had been kept. They lowered themselves into it by ropes and made off into the night. The news of the outrage spread to the town. Summoned by the tocsin, the citizens of Edinburgh, their provost at their head, arrived with torches and arms in the outer court of the Palace. They asked to see the Queen. This was not allowed.

Mary was guarded by eighty Douglas cut-throats who refused to allow her any speech, even with her own servants. Now they promised to cut her into pieces if she showed herself at a window. Darnley from a window pacified the townspeople.

Long before midnight, then, it seemed that the conspirators had won a remarkable victory. Only in one respect had it fallen short of their hopes: Bothwell and Huntly were at large. With that important exception, all the omens were favourable. The Queen's power would now be limited by Act of Parliament. Probably she would be imprisoned in Stirling Castle. Darnley would be invested with full royal powers. Moray could safely return from banishment. (He did so on the day after the murder.) The Protestant religion would be safeguarded. And Riccio was dead.

While the citizens outside murmured and the conspirators watched within, the Italian's body was stripped and washed for burial in the porter's lodge on a small wooden chest. 'This was his destiny,' said the porter, 'for on this chest was his first bed when he came to this place.'

When he heard of the night's work John Knox exclaimed that it was beyond all praise.

Riding through day and night from Edinburgh to Berwick, to York, to London, Queen Elizabeth's couriers carried dispatches with a superscription that commanded all speed and summoned the best horses: 'Haste, haste, post haste, haste. For life, for life, for life!'

Wearing a portrait of Mary on a gold chain hanging from her waist, the Queen told the Spanish ambassador, Guzman de Silva, that, had she been in Mary's place on the night of the murder, she would have stabbed her husband with his own dagger. Never, never would she see Darnley again.

What Mary did on the day after the murder was different and more ingenious. Choking back her hatred of her husband, she set herself to win him over. It was folly, she told him, to suppose that he could trust his new confederates. Meanwhile Mary reached Bothwell with a messenger. The Queen's arguments, pursued on every opportunity that Sunday, prevailed on Monday morning. Darnley arranged a grim little farce in which Mary 'forgave' the three chief rebels, Morton, Ruthven and Lindsay, who knelt on the floor of her chamber, still stained by Riccio's blood. With many misgivings, the conspirators withdrew their garrison from the Palace, and the ringleaders went off to supper at Morton's town house.

The moment they had left the Palace, Mary ordered horses from John Stewart of Traquair. A few minutes before midnight she led Darnley through the pantry, where all the servants were French and could therefore be trusted, to a door leading out to the Abbey burial ground. Twelve was striking as they passed the new-made grave in which Riccio's body lay. It is said that Mary paused in order to pour out curses on her husband's family, the house of Lennox. This does not seem probable, although Mary may well have made secret vows of revenge as she stole past in the moonlight.

Close at hand, holding the heads of four horses, were Stewart of Traquair and Mary's Master of Horse, Arthur Erskine. Six riders mounted, Mary behind Erskine. They rode eastwards to Seton, ten miles away, where, by arrangement, Bothwell's patrols were on the look-out for them. After a short consultation the Queen decided to continue her journey to Dunbar Castle, a bleak royal fortress on the rocky Lothian coast. There they arrived as dawn was breaking. Mary immediately set about making breakfast.

By her cunning, her histrionic gift, the feminine charm she could exert at will, her courage, and by a physical endurance, which in the circumstances was extraordinary, she had turned the tables completely on the rebellion. Without the command of the Queen's person, Morton, Ruthven and their associates were deprived of their chief political asset. And now between them and Darnley, who a few hours before had been their ally and creature, there yawned a pit of hatred and distrust. Darnley, who had betrayed them, knew that he could count on their unappeasable thirst for revenge.

Bothwell made off in haste to drum up fighting men from the unruly Borders; soon he returned to Dunbar at the head of 4000 horse. Soon two of the rebel earls, Glencairn and Rothes, rode up to the gates of Mary's castle to surrender. Recognising defeat when they saw it, Morton, Lindsay and Ruthven took their several ways southward to England. John Knox, having applauded those who had advised taking 'just punishment on that knave David', lost no time in leaving Edinburgh for the west country.

The *coup d'état*, after so auspicious an opening, had collapsed.

The abrupt reversal of political fortune in Scotland was accomplished by a woman of twenty-five who was expecting her first child in three months' time, and who had just been the witness, by eye and ear, of the brutal murder of her most trusted servant.

News of the affair spread across Europe, giving rise to all sorts of rumours and alarms. Queen Elizabeth wrote to the Warden of the English Middle Marches ordering the Scottish fugitives 'out of our realm'. Morton, pleading shortage of funds, was allowed to stay.

The Pope sent Mary his congratulations: 'We were struck with horror when we heard of the danger in which you were, owing to the treason of heretics. But the joy we felt was greater still when we heard of your noted valour, your greatness of soul and admirable constancy . . . we shall therefore immediately send you money, not indeed as much as we should wish, but as much as we can—we shall also send an apostolic Nuncio.' Mary's envoy in Rome, the Bishop of Dunblane, was invited by the Holy Father to a notably meagre supper. 'I restrict myself,' the Pope explained, 'in order to have the more with which to aid your queen.'

Mary rode back to Edinburgh guarded by four companies of professional soldiers and a cavalcade of Border horse. Bothwell rode at the head of the little army. The citizens of Edinburgh, as if anxious to make up to the Queen for their failure to rescue her from the conspirators, escorted her in strength to the Bishop of Dunkeld's house in the Cowgate. To the annoyance of many, the Queen ordered that Riccio should have a handsome tomb in the Abbey church at Holyrood. And she appointed in his place as her French secretary Riccio's seventeen-year-old brother Joseph, who had arrived in Scotland in the suite of a French envoy, Castelnau de Mauvissière. It was a defiant, rather than a wise, appointment.

Darnley, by this time a subject of universal contempt, signed a declaration of his complete innocence of any part in the recent conspiracy, which was displayed at the Cross of Edinburgh. Nobody believed it. His betrayed accomplices in the murder plot waited for revenge. In the meantime, Mary allowed the poor wretch no part whatever in state affairs.

On the 19th June, in Edinburgh Castle, Mary's son was born. When Darnley called to see the child, Mary said, 'My Lord, God has given you and me a child, begotten by none but you. Here I protest to God, as I shall answer to him on the great day of judgment, this is your son, and no other man's. He is so much your son that I fear it will be the worse for him.'

Blushing, Darnley replied, 'Sweet Madam, is this your promise to forgive and forget all?'

'I have forgiven all,' she retorted, 'but I will never forget. What if Fawdonside's pistol had fired? What would have become of the child and me?'

'Madam,' said Darnley, 'these things are all past.'

Four days later, Sir James Melville, who had ridden hard all the way, arrived in London with the news of the birth. Elizabeth was dancing in the hall at Greenwich Palace when Cecil brought her the message. It is said that, for a little, the Queen was caught off guard. It is said—and surely these words, if any, have the true Elizabethan ring—that she broke out to her ladies, 'The Queen of Scots is lighter of a fair son, while I am but a barren stock!' There was no more dancing at Greenwich that night. Next morning, when Elizabeth received Melville in audience, she was at her most sprightly.

Mary's son was christened at the hour of vespers, on Sunday, 17th September, 1566, in the Chapel Royal at Stirling, the Privy Council having loosened the purse strings so far as to vote £12,000 for the pageantry that marked the occasion. The baby's cloth of estate was of bright crimson velvet trimmed with gold. Its bedspread needed ten yards of cloth of silver. The Queen's horses were caprisoned in gold with silver fringes. And the retinue of each noble wore livery of a colour which Mary herself had chosen. The foreign guests were equally magnificent.

The French ambassador, the Comte de Brienne, who was to carry the child to the font, gave Mary a diamond chain and pendant. Elizabeth's representative, the Earl of Bedford, was accompanied by eighty horsemen and brought as the gift of his mistress a huge gold font.

Bedford, like Bothwell and Moray, observed the popish ceremony from the chapel door, a circumstance that was in due course sourly noted in a letter to Rome: 'He being a Calvinist, would not assist at the holy ceremony, but begged the bastard sister of the Queen of Scotland, the Countess of Argyll, to whom he gave a diamond worth five hundred scudi, to take part therein on behalf of the Queen of England.'

The ceremony was conducted with full Catholic rites by the Archbishop of St. Andrews whom Mary had not long before called a 'poxy priest'. The adjective was not lightly used. The Primate had lately spent 1800 gold crowns on treatment from Dr. Jerome Cardan of Milan.

After the christening of the new Prince as James Charles, Duke of Rothesay, Earl of Carrick, Kyle and Cunningham, there followed several days of festivities for sixty distinguished guests—banquets, masques, a bull-fight, and a ballet of nymphs and satyrs designed by the Queen's French valet Sebastien Pages.

This last entertainment greatly annoyed an English visitor, Christopher Hatton, one of Elizabeth's Gentleman Pensioners. He was a tall, good-looking young lawyer from Northamptonshire who, two years before, had caught his queen's eye by his graceful dancing in a masque at Gray's Inn.

When the satyrs in the hall of Stirling Castle provocatively wagged their tails, Hatton had no doubt at all that this was an offensive reference to the legend, widely believed outside England, that all Englishmen were born with tails. He said that, were it not for the Queen's presence, he would stab that French knave Bastien to the heart. He and Mr. Lignish, who had come as the Duke of

Norfolk's representative, sat on the floor with their backs to the insulting performance.

The worst blot on the occasion was, however, the absence of Darnley, the King, father of the baby Prince. He sulked in his room in the castle, refusing to attend the christening or to take part in any of the festivities. He was treated with the contempt his surliness had invited. His silver plate was removed to grace the banquet table; he ate off pewter. It was believed that the Queen had cut down his spending money. He began a recitation of his grievances to the French ambassador, who, in the end, said that his apartment had two doors and he would leave by one as Darnley entered by the other. The ambassador's opinion was that Darnley's bad behaviour was incurable. Writing from Paris, Vincenzo Laureo, the Papal Nuncio to Scotland, reported to the Cardinal of Alessandria, that Darnley 'never appeared at any public ceremony but remained almost always in retirement in his lodging, and seldom went abroad beyond the town to amuse himself, and then with a very small train'.

By his conduct, the King had fastened a deadly insult on his wife. He had proclaimed, in the plainest and most public manner, in the face of foreign ambassadors, the nobility and the commons, his opinion that James, Prince and High Steward of Scotland, Duke of Rothesay, was a bastard. It is unlikely that Darnley believed anything of the sort; in which case, his conduct to his wife was all the more unforgivable.

Stuart and Guise, with the pride of the one in her veins and the ferocity of the other, Mary was not likely to forgive quickly or at all. And there were not lacking others ready to keep the fires of hatred blazing between husband and wife. As the Papal Nuncio wrote anxiously to Rome, 'Their quarrel is constantly nourished and increased by the malice of a few powerful rebels, and very seriously disturbs public business, especially the restoration of holy religion in that kingdom.' The reverend Nuncio looked with an almost despairing eye on the news which reached him from Scotland, that far-off land which he was destined never to see. 'Surely,' he cried, 'there is need of the special aid of God our Lord. May He deign to bend and regulate the unquiet mind of that too boyish prince!'

Darnley was no match for his wife in quickness of wit or histrionic talent. But instinct told him that some unpleasant event was being prepared of which he was to be the victim. He was not wrong.

In the little castle of Craigmillar, just south of Edinburgh, Mary had spent a few days a month before the christening, discussing with Bothwell, Moray, Lethington, Huntly and Argyll the wreck of her marriage. What was to be done? Divorce? But would the Church recognise it? Annulment? In that case her son would have no claim to the throne.

Bothwell thought the matter could be arranged without prejudice to the Prince's rights. After all, his own mother and father had been divorced, yet he had succeeded to the title. Lethington, too, was reassuring: 'We shall find a way by which your grace shall be quit of him without prejudice to your son. Although Lord Moray here is as scrupulous a Protestant as your grace is a Papist, I am sure he will look through his fingers and behold our doings, saying nothing.'

Darnley's behaviour at Stirling gave additional urgency to the business. There was more than boorishness to complain of. William Hiegate, the town clerk of Glasgow, spread a story which reached Mary's ears: Darnley meant to throw her into prison and crown the baby Prince as King so that he, Darnley, might rule as Regent. The Queen could find no confirmation of the rumour.

But, in one form or another, it was continually cropping up. Even in Paris, the Archbishop of Glasgow, her ambassador, heard a whisper from the Spanish ambassador which caused him to send a Scottish Archer to Edinburgh to warn Mary that 'some surprise' against her was in the making. She should cause the captain of her guard to be diligent.

Before the advice reached Mary—before even the Archbishop penned it—Darnley had retired to Glasgow, a stronghold of his family. What he might have done next is a matter of conjecture. In those days, the young man's head was full of wild and romantic ideas, conceived in a sick brain and hatched by violent resentment. When Darnley felt himself slighted, when he dreamed grandiose dreams of winning a position in the world befitting him as a Prince of the Blood, as the husband of a queen, as a titular king, as a Catholic nobleman, he had at his elbow young men almost as hot-headed as himself to egg him on. His closest companions about this time were two English Catholics each named Anthony Standen.

One of the Standen brothers, the elder, lived to become an associate of the Gunpowder Plot conspirators a generation later.

Pride, vanity, and recklessness—in this unhealthy atmosphere Darnley wove his crazy, insubstantial webs. He sought to convince the Spaniards that he would make a more reliable and energetic Catholic monarch for Scotland than his wife. He thought of attacking Scarborough and raising the Papists of the North against Queen Elizabeth. He talked of seizing the Scilly Islands and holding them against England as an advanced base for a Spanish fleet.

Perhaps these fancies were simply the forerunners of the disease that now struck him down, with a high fever and other unpleasant symptoms. Either Darnley had contracted smallpox or, as seems more likely, syphilis.

Mary sent her doctor to him and offered to visit him. Darnley answered by word of mouth and with bitterness: if Glasgow were Lord Bothwell's castle of the Hermitage and if he were Bothwell, he had no doubt she would quickly be with him, undesired.

On January 20, 1567, Mary set off from Edinburgh to visit her sick husband. Bothwell rode with her as far as Callendar, Lord Livingstone's house near Falkirk.

Sometime during that autumn and winter Mary had fallen passionately in love with the Lord High Admiral of Scotland, Lieutenant of the Border, the returned exile, James Hepburn, Earl of Bothwell. The fact is plain; the reason is obscure.

Ever since the event, historians have thrown themselves into convulsions of perplexity to account for so strange and unnatural a passion as Mary's. As if the world was not full of examples of beautiful women falling under the spell of enterprising men of bad character who have not even looks to commend them!

Only a few months before, Mary had found a bride for Bothwell. It was a symptom of her interest and maybe of her benevolence. It may even have made him more tempting to her. Mary was not simply a young woman with the beat of passion in her veins; she was a sovereign, above the law, herself the embodiment of the law, one who looked on the young men of her court with a possessive or, at least, a speculative gaze, and had not the psychological barriers behind which the sexual instincts of her cousin Elizabeth fretted.

Bothwell belonged to a breed of bold, acquisitive, and unscrupulous men common enough in that age. Women, jewels, lands, fame and power, these were the prizes they sought by displaying a well-shaped calf, turning a dexterous sonnet or allowing an insolent glance to linger a second too long in a woman's eyes. By intrigue, by the dagger, by some spectacular extravagance, by winning the favour of men or women, particularly women of high position, they made their way in the dangerous world, treading warily the path between semi-royal state and the scaffold.

Lacking some of their polish and splendour, Bothwell was of the breed of Leicester, Essex, Hatton, De Vere, or of Mary's uncle, François, Duc de Guise, a noble grander than any of these—and at least as ugly as Bothwell—but one who, like them, owed his extraordinary position in France to the exercise of personal influence with a monarch.

François had captivated Henri II and, through his beautiful Scottish niece, Mary Stuart, had dominated Henri's son, Mary's first husband, François II. He had ruled France, king in all but name. Perhaps he dreamed of the crown, as his brother Charles, the Cardinal, dreamed of the Papal Tiara. A slight turn in the religious-political struggle in France might have brought the reality.

When Bothwell returned from a raid upon some Border miscreants, wounded in face and hand, as he did a few weeks after the christening at Stirling, Mary may have been reminded of 'Scarface', as Guise was called after a lance-thrust full in the cheek had marked him for life. In any case, it was less important that Bothwell was ugly, coarse, with a reputation none too savoury, than that he was an impetuous man of action.

Given the nature of Mary's two marriages, the first pathetic, the second wretched, the first to a sickly, impotent boy, the second to a degenerate youth, it is hardly surprising that there was more haste than wisdom about her infatuation with Bothwell.

Given Mary's feelings about Darnley, the physical disgust, the emotional revulsion, the contempt, Bothwell was the kind of man in whom her eye alighting one day, discerned an appeal of which she had not been aware. He was, as it turned out, the one great passion of her life. A passion brief, maybe, but none the less calamitous.

Bothwell looked on the Queen with an eye in which there was more covetousness than love. Mary was the supreme sexual prize of the age. She was also a queen with favours to bestow. In Scotland, Bothwell walked by himself among the nobility, despised by the heads of the greater families—Douglas, Hamilton, Gordon, Campbell and the rest—and hating them in return. Through Mary he might win the right to despise them too.

5 No recipe against fear

WHEN MARY SET OUT on that extraordinary and disastrous journey to Glasgow it is unlikely that she had any final, fixed idea what she was going to do when she arrived there. She had loved her husband, seizing on that love as if it were her last chance in life, showering gifts on Darnley as if she were a rich old woman desperately trying to buy a young man's favour with glittering stones, gleaming horses, soft, resplendent clothes, titles. But she was not old. Her startling beauty had not begun to fade. It had not vanished twenty years later, when death was brought into the room at Fotheringay after waiting so long, patiently, outside.

She had been in love with him, blind to his follies, wild to chain him to her and with a quality of crazy self-assertion in her passion, strange in a woman who had felt so many vibrations of men's desire around her. There was, in all likelihood, resentment of Elizabeth, some defiance of the rival, in her lavishness to Darnley. Perhaps, too, there was also the wish to convince herself of her love for Darnley. Mary, living so much in that private world which her desires and her will dyed so strongly with their light, had a majestic power of self-deception. To marry Darnley had been dynastically brilliant, politically astute, a wonderfully telling blow against the woman in London. Upon this luxuriant soil Mary's love for Darnley flourished until she believed that it was real. And then one day it was no longer there.

To Darnley, who had never loved her, the humiliation of this discovery was no doubt the sharper. Having given her a child, he was thrown away, an empty vessel, as if he belonged to one of those species in which the male is devoured by the female as soon as he has fulfilled his function and fertilised her. Some of the blame for Darnley's brutish misconduct may be pinned upon the mere jealousy of the rejected male. He found himself shut first out of the Queen's council and then out of the woman's bed. He repaid her non-love with his enmity.

Then came the night when her coldness to him clotted into hatred, when he and the men who had duped him snatched the Queen's toy from her and smashed it before her eyes, within her hearing, on the floor at Holyrood. The night of Riccio's murder.

But even after that hideous event, Mary's rage against the man did not burn with a steady flame. There were moments—the endless, fruitless conferences at Craigmillar prove it—when she realised that she was chained to Darnley and could only free herself at the risk of destroying herself; moments, in short, when Mary, who had once thought herself into love, almost thought herself into love again.

It seems likely that one of the motives, unavowed and no doubt hardly formed, that sent her riding westwards across Scotland in that iron January of 1567 was to see what, if anything, could be saved of her marriage with Darnley. The question—if one can call by such a name anything so frail and secretive—was not, of course, the admitted purpose of the expedition.

Mary was going to visit a husband who had nearly died and who was still sick. She was going to ask him what he meant to do—fly from Scotland and plot against her? Flee to Spain and plot against both her and Elizabeth? Stay in Scotland and, with accomplices, throw her into prison so that he could reign in her place as regent for their son—until ambition took him one step further still? This had been Darnley's aim on the night of Riccio's murder. Had he now given up the perilous and bloody dream?

Mary went well accompanied on the westward ride across Scotland—surrounded by a troop of well-armed, well-mounted arquebusiers picked by Bothwell and in her pay. Even so, the ride was not without its dangers. Glasgow was in the heart of the Lennox country where the word of Darnley's father might carry more authority than that of Darnley's wife. She went to Glasgow over all else because, in the unfinished, secret war between her and the Queen of England, she must know what was in the mind of the young man whom, in an audacious challenge to Elizabeth, she had married.

It is possible that Mary, whose intuitive gift was for action, never followed the intricacies of her English cousin's attitude. The duplicities. The ambivalences, knotted together like the ends of threads: The nervous tics and deadly dangers of the duel between two sovereigns. The intense, bitter curiosity that one woman felt about the other woman—is she more beautiful; does she dance more elegantly; can she make music as skilfully as I?—and refused ever to gratify by a personal encounter. The virgin's veto on her cousin's marriage—and the foreknowledge that Mary's child, fruit of the forbidden union, would be her heir.

How strange a part Mary was to play in the life of the other and, one must say, the greater woman! To be the most sedulous threat to her life and work, the presence, innocent or knowing, behind the dagger of every assassin—and to furnish, out of her own body, the solution to the one riddle Elizabeth could not solve, the succession to the English throne! To end under the axe wielded by Elizabeth's servant—and to launch the life that would continue Elizabeth's reign!

To believe that, riding, heavily mantled within her hedge of horsemen, across that landscape denuded by winter, its hills black and dappled blue, lying off near the horizon and huddled against the brown clouds, the lochs, shields of forbidding water whipped by the wind, the daunting sudden panorama of the winter sea—to believe that there was some fixed resolution in Mary's mind of what she would do and how it should be done—that is to ask too much of belief. To ask too much of Mary, whose imagination at best gave out a broken and smoky light.

She may not even have measured the danger that was every day rising higher around her, although she was aware of the tightening grip of the European religious war. Rome, Paris, her family in France, the Jesuits who came stealthily into her country—they expected more, much more from her than she could give. There were moments of revulsion—and she was near one now—when she was ready to throw up the whole impossible task she had inherited.

She was, too, in love with Bothwell, desperately and submissively. There is something at once pathetic and frightening in the way this proud, desirable young woman acknowledged her lover as her master. For he was reckless, with plenty of boldness but little finesse. And he would take her along a path where dangers thickened.

For half of this distance, that is, as far as Lord Livingstone's house, Mary was accompanied by Bothwell and Huntly. After spending a night there she completed the journey alone.

On the road, not far from Glasgow, probably on January 22, the cavalcade pulled up. An emissary from the Earl of Lennox, Captain Thomas Crawford, greeted the Queen and made his master's excuses for not attending on her. The reason was not that his lordship was unaware of his duty as a subject but that his health was indifferent. Besides, she had spoken sharply about him to his servant, Robert Cunningham, at Stirling, and he did not dare to enter her presence until he knew better what were her feelings about him.

Mary retorted scornfully, 'There is no recipe against fear. And he would not be afraid were he not guilty.'

Crawford—as he described the interview later—replied that his lordship wished that the secrets of every creature's heart were written in their face.

The insinuation was not wasted on the Queen. She asked Crawford sharply if he had any further commission to carry out.

'No.'

'Very well, hold your peace.'

With no more ado, Mary rode forward into Glasgow, a pleasant little village on the river Clyde, gathered around a superb cathedral.

The clergy buildings had suffered through the zeal of the Reformers. The Archbishop's Palace—official residence of Mary's Ambassador then in Paris—stood empty. She seems to have made it her headquarters during the few days she spent in the town. Nearby, in the Castle, lay Darnley and his father Lennox, invalids. The Glasgow streets and closes were unusually full—of armed men owing their allegiance to the Lennox connection or to the Hamiltons, their deadly enemies. In addition to the protection given her by her own bodyguard, Mary could count on the safety factor that was derived from the rough balance of the rival feudal forces in the town.

The beginning and the conclusion of the Queen's visit to her husband can be stated in a few words and are not in doubt. She went to his bedside, found him convalescent. After several interviews he returned with her to Edinburgh on a horse litter which she had brought with her for the purpose. There are two accounts of the discussions between husband and wife.

One is by Thomas Crawford, written nearly two years after the event and purporting to give Darnley's version of what passed. The other is, on the face of it, Mary's own record in a letter written by her in Glasgow and sent by hand to Lord Bothwell. Did the Queen really write it in anything resembling the form in which it exists? Was it forged or tampered with so as to injure Mary's reputation?

The age was one in which forgery—like assassination—flourished as a political art. Nor should it be assumed that, because Scotland was impoverished and backward, it lacked the native talent, adequate ingenuity, experience and perfidy to trump up a document in order to serve some major end of policy. And there could hardly be a more important object of statecraft in the year 1567, in Scotland or in England either, than the personal credit of the Queen of Scots. Mary's good name may not, indeed, stand or fall on the authenticity of a single document. But the letter is an impressive item in the dossier.

This is the moment when it is necessary to take account of what is known in history, for reasons that will later appear, as the Second of the Casket Letters.

6 The place shall hold unto death

THE LETTER IS LONG: more than 3000 words. In its original form it was almost certainly in French. The original no longer exists. Contemporary translations into Scots, English and Latin have survived. There is also a re-translation of the Scottish version into French.

Concocted or genuine, the letter is a remarkable one by any standard. Its immediate relevance is that it gives a coherent account and explanation of events which are known to have taken place: Mary's journey to Glasgow; her visit to her sick husband; their return together to Edinburgh. For the present, it will be assumed that it was written by the Queen of Scots.

The letter opens abruptly, with a long sentence of a certain rhetorical splendour.

'Being departed from the place where I left my heart,' says the Queen, in the Scottish version of the letter, which is modernised and anglicised here, 'it is easy to judge what was my countenance, seeing that I was like a body without a heart; which was the reason that until dinner time I talked to nobody, nor yet dared any present themselves to me, judging it was not good to do so.'

She then tells of the encounter with Crawford, four miles out of Glasgow, and of their talk, concluding, 'Summa, I made him hold his tongue, the rest were long to tell.'

After that she was met by Sir James Hamilton, the Laird of Luss, and other gentlemen, with about forty horse. 'Never one of the townspeople came to speak to me, which causes me to think that they are his' (i.e. on the side of Lennox and Darnley) . . . 'I see no other gentleman but those of my company.' The writer then passes to more intimate matters.

'The King sent for Joachim last night and asked why I did not lodge near him and that he would rise' (from his sick bed) 'the sooner if that were so and for what reason had I come—was it for an amicable settlement?

'In particular, were you' (i.e. Bothwell) 'there? And if I had settled the officers of my household, if I had taken Paris' (as her chamberlain) 'and Gilbert to write' (i.e. to act as her secretary) 'and that I would send Joseph away . . . I am amazed who has told him so much. Yes, he spoke even of the marriage of Bastien.'[1]

At this point, the letter changes in theme and, without warning, becomes an account of Mary's first interview with her husband.

'I asked him about his letters in which he had complained of the cruelty of some people. [He] answered that he was [rêvoit] in a daze, and that he was so happy to see me that he believed he would die for gladness; he found it a great fault in me that I was pensive.

'I went to supper. He begged me to return, which I did. He told me about his illness and said that he would make no will but only leave everything to me—and that I was the cause of his malady because of the regret he had that I was alienated from him.

' "You ask me," he said, "what I mean in my letters when I speak of cruelty. It is of your cruelty alone that will not accept my offers and repentance. I confess that I have done wrong, but not the thing which I have always denied; as so likewise have many of your subjects transgressed, which you have forgiven them.

' "I am young. You will say that you have forgiven me many times and yet I return to my sins. May not any man of my age fall twice or thrice, for lack of advice or by breaking his promise, and at last repent and be chastened by experience?

' "If I may obtain pardon, I protest that I shall never disappoint again. And I crave nothing but that we may be at bed and board together as husband and wife. And if you will not, I will never rise out of this bed. I pray you tell me what you mean to do. God knows how I am punished for having made my god of you and for having no other thought but of you. And if at any time I offend you, you

---

1. Joachim, Nicholas Hubert, known as Paris, and Gilbert Curle were all servants of Mary's. Joseph Riccio, brother of David, was her secretary until he was dismissed. Bastien Pages was about to marry the Queen's maid and did so in Holyrood, three weeks later. It is obvious, then, that Darnley was well informed about what was going on in the Queen's immediate circle.

are the cause of it, because when anybody does me any wrong, if I find relief in complaining to you, I carry my grievance to no one else. But when I hear something, and am not on familiar terms with you, necessity constrains me to keep it in my breast and that causes me to lose my wits out of sheer anger." '

Mary asked why he meant to leave in the English ship. This Darnley denied, on his word, that he had intended to do, although he admitted he had spoken to the sailors. He denied that there was any truth in Hiegate's story of his plot to seize the Queen and crown her son as King. But when Mary quoted his own reported words to him, Darnley changed his tune. He said that the Laird of Minto, Lord Provost of Glasgow and a Lennox adherent, had sent him word that some members of the Queen's council had brought her a letter for her signature ordering Darnley to be put in prison and slain if he resisted.

'Tomorrow,' the writer says, 'I will speak to him upon this point. The rest of Willie Hiegate's story he confessed, but it was the morning after my arrival that he did so.'

In the end, Darnley pressed her to stay with him. Mary refused: 'I said to him that he must be purged' (of his infection) 'and that could not be done here. He said to me, "I hear you have brought a litter with you but I would rather travel with you." I believe he thought I would send him away a prisoner. I answered that I would take him with me to Craigmillar where the doctor and I might help him and not be far from my son. He answered that he was ready when I pleased, provided I would promise to grant him his wish. He has no desire to be seen and becomes angry when I speak to him about Walker[1] and says that he will pluck his ears out of his head and that he lies.

'For I asked him before about that, and what cause he had to complain about some of the lords and threaten them. He denies that and says he loves them all and begs me to give credence to nothing against him. As for me, he would rather give his life than cause me any displeasure. And after this he showed me so many little flatteries so seriously and so wisely that you would be amazed.

'I had almost forgotten that he said he could not doubt me in this story of Hiegate's for he would never believe that I, who was his

1. Through whom Hiegate's story first reached Mary.

own flesh, would do him any evil and besides it was shown that I had refused to sign it.[1]

'But, as to any others who might pursue him, at least he could sell his life dearly enough—but he suspected nobody and would not but love everybody I loved. He would not let me leave him but wanted me to sit up with him. I made it appear that I believed everything he says is true. And that I will think about it. And I excused myself, saying that I could not sit up with him that night.

'He said he did not sleep well: you never saw him better, nor speak more humbly. And, if I had not proof that his heart was of wax and that mine was not like a diamond wherein no shot can make a breach but that which comes forth of your hand, I would almost have had pity on him. But, fear not, the place shall hold unto the death! Remember, in return for that, not to allow yours to be won by that false race that would do no less to yourself.

'I believe they have been at school together. He has always the tear in his eye. He salutes everybody, yes, even to the meanest, and makes piteous caressing of them that they may take pity on him. Today his father bled at the mouth and nose—guess what that may presage. I have not yet seen him. He keeps to his room. The King wants me to give him food with my own hands. But do not be more trustful where you are than I shall do here.

'This is my first day. I shall finish tomorrow. I write everything, of no matter how little consequence, so that you may select from the whole what is best for your purpose.

'I am doing here a work I greatly detest. Does it not make you wish to laugh to see me lie so well or at least dissemble so well and now and again tell him the truth . . . You have heard the rest. We are coupled with two false races, the devil separates us. God knit us together forever as most faithful couple that ever He united. This my faith, I will die in it.

'Excuse me if I write badly. You must guess half of it. But I cannot improve it because I am ill at ease since I cannot sleep as they do and as I would desire, that is, in your arms, my dear life, whom I pray God to preserve from all ill and send you repose. I am going to seek mine until the morning when I shall end my bible.[2] But I

1. The order for Darnley's imprisonment.
2. Perhaps a mis-reading of the French '*mon billet*'. More likely a half-humorous reference to the length of the letter.

am annoyed that it should hinder me from writing news of myself to you, because it is so long.

'Let me know what you have decided to do in the matter you know about, so that we may understand each other's mind and in consequence nothing may go amiss.

'I am weary and going to sleep and yet I cannot stop scribbling as long as there is paper left.

'Cursed be this poxy fellow that causes me all this trouble for I had a pleasanter subject to discourse on. He is not too much disfigured yet he has had a bad attack. He has almost slain me with his breath; it is worse than your uncle's; and yet I came no nearer to him than in a chair at the bedfoot, and he being at the other end of it.'

At this point, it seems, the pen did at last fall from the sleepy writer's hand. There follows in the text a memorandum of ten items, most of which had been already dealt with. It seems, then, that whoever wrote the letter ran out of paper and, writing in haste and late at night, used a sheet on which the notes had been written. This is referred to towards the end of the second half of the letter:

'Excuse the thing that is scribbled for I had no paper yesterday when I wrote on the paper of the memorial.'

Apparently the 'memorial' was under the writer's eye when the letter was resumed, for she picks up the final item on the list, 'Of Monsieur de Livingstone': and speaks of an incident at Callendar which she had forgotten to mention in the earlier part of the letter:

'At supper he' (Lord Livingstone) 'said in the Lady Reres's[1] ear that he would drink to the folk I know of if I would pledge them. And after supper he said to me when I was leaning against him warming myself at the fire, "You have fair going to see fine folk, yet you cannot be so welcome to them as you have this day left somebody regretful who will never be blithe until he sees you again!" I asked him who that was. With that he nudged me and said that some of his folk had seen your annoyance.

'You may guess the rest.'

There follow a few sentences about a bracelet which the writer has been making so that it could be sent with the letter and which she begs the recipient to hide since everyone has seen her making it.

1. Wife of Arthur Forbes of Reres, a confidante of Mary's.

She then turns abruptly to what she calls 'my tiresome remarks'. They are, in fact, if they are authentic, the most revealing and tragic sentences in the letter:

'You make me dissemble so far that I have a horror of it and you cause me almost to play the part of a traitress. Remember, were it not that I am obeying you, I had rather be dead than do it. My heart bleeds for it.

'Summa[1], he will not come with me except on condition that I will promise to be at bed and board with him as before, and that I shall not leave him afterwards; and that, having given him my word, he will do everything as I please and come with me. But he has prayed me to stay with him until the day after tomorrow.'

When Darnley pressed her on the matter of resuming married life together, she agreed ('for to make him trust me I must deceive him in some things') but told him to tell nobody of their intention. For the nobles would be afraid that he would then carry out the threats he had uttered to make them pay, were he ever reconciled with Mary, for their contemptuous treatment of him. They knew that Darnley had advised her not to court them at his expense and they would be jealous were she, suddenly, without consulting them, to change sides.

To this Darnley replied 'very joyfully':

'And think you they will esteem you the more for that! But I believe at present that you want us to live together in tranquillity. For if it were otherwise, greater inconvenience might come to us both than we are aware of. But now I will do whatever you will do and will love all that you love and wish you to make them love me likewise, for since they do not seek my life, I love them all equally . . .'

'Summa,' says the writer, passing to a more sinister topic, 'he will go anywhere on my word. Alas, I never deceived anybody. But I remit myself altogether to your will. Send me word what I shall do and whatever comes of it, I will obey you. Consider too if you can find out any more secret invention by medicine for he is to take medicine and the bath[2] at Craigmillar. He may not come out of the house for a long time.

'Summa, by all that I can learn, he is highly suspicious and yet,

1. Translation of *en somme*.
2. A bath would be the final stage in Darnley's cure.

notwithstanding, he trusts my word. But as yet not so far that he will disclose anything to me. But nevertheless, I shall draw it out of him. I shall never rejoice to deceive anyone that believes in me. Yet, notwithstanding, you may command me in all things. Have no bad opinion of me on that account, because you are the occasion of it yourself, because for my own particular revenge I would not do it to him.'

A few sentences follow in which the writer speaks of Darnley's nagging suspicions of her conduct:

'Summa, for certainty he fears the thing you know of, and for his life. But as to that, I had only to speak two or three good words to him and he was happy, his doubts dispelled. I did not see him this evening in the hope of finishing your bracelet for which I can get no clasps.... Let me know if you want to have it and if you want more money and when I shall return and how far I may speak ... He desires me to come and see him rise in the morning early ... Burn this letter for it is too dangerous and nothing in it is well expressed, for I am thinking of nothing but troubles ...

'Now, seeing that to obey you, my dear love, I spare neither honour, conscience, hazard nor greatness whatsoever, take it, I pray you, in good part and not according to interpretation of your false brother-in-law[1] to whom I pray you give no credit against the most faithful lover that ever you had or ever shall have. See not her[2] whose feigned tears should not be so praised or esteemed as the true and faithful travail which I endure in order to merit her place. For obtaining the which against my nature I betray them who might prevent me.

'God forgive me and God give you, my only love, the fortune and prosperity which your humble and faithful love desires you who hopes to be shortly another thing to you, for the reward of my irksome pains.

'It is late. I desire never to cease from writing to you yet now, after kissing your hands, I will end my letter. Excuse my bad writing, and read it twice over. Excuse the thing that is scribbled, for I had no paper yesterday when I wrote on the paper of the memorial. Remember your love and write to her and that very often. Love me as I shall love you.'

1. Lord Huntly.
2. Lady Bothwell.

The letter closes with another memorandum of half a dozen items. There is no signature.

The narrative of the events of January 1567 must be interrupted at this point to consider what value is to be attached to the Second of the Casket Letters, as it is called. One thing can be said at once without fear of denial. Whether the letter belongs to history or to imaginative literature, whether it is the outpouring of an over-wrought young woman at the crisis of a passionate love affair, or the calculated but inspired invention of a fiction-writer of genius, it is a psychological document of incomparable interest.

How wonderfully the play of conscience and passion over a woman's mind are conveyed by those breathless sentences! How exactly, too, is reflected that mental state which will be familiar to anyone who has loved deeply, where the writer longs, through exhaustion, to bring the letter to an end but is driven on from idea to idea by the obsession to continue speaking, through pen and paper, to the beloved!

The writer speaks of her haste and weariness but, in truth, there is no need to do so. They are implicit in the slack linking of one thought to its successor by a frequently repeated 'and'. She asks to be excused for 'my evil writing', as Mary Stuart does several times in letters which have never been disputed as hers.

If the letter belongs to fiction, it is not simply a feat of forgery. *That* it could certainly be; a forgery skilful enough to imitate Mary's hand to the Scottish Privy Council which contained friends of hers as well as enemies, and each member of which would be familiar with her handwriting. However, the Italian hand in which Mary wrote could possibly have been confused by men accustomed to another style of writing, with similar writing by another person. There might have been interpolations. There might have been forgery. One point, however, must be noted. The forgery would, of necessity, conform not only to the Queen's hand in general but to her calligraphy as exhaustion progressively affected it.

In the Scotland of the sixteenth century there might well have been clever forgers. There were certainly men whom no scruple would impede from forgery in what they might see as a worthy and urgent cause—blackening the name of a leading antagonist in politics. A man like George Buchanan, for example, who spread calumnies about Mary, might well have stooped to forgery against her. All that can be said is that a truly exceptional degree of skill in counterfeiting would have been called for and that, then or later, no individual has been plausibly suspected of the crime.

However, there is something more subtle involved than any mere imitation of handwriting. There is the fact that the letter is written round one set of memoranda and finishes with another. The most brilliant counterfeiter in the world would hardly have stumbled upon such inventions, so natural as they happened, and yet, as he would be bound to think, so disconcerting if they were contrived.

There is also a question of style. As a woman of strongly individual temperament, Mary had her own way of expressing herself. She had been brought up in France and wrote French more readily than Scots. The letter is full of examples of French idiom which seem to have been translated more or less literally into Scots.

Either Mary was thinking in French as she wrote, or the original letter was in French and what is before us is a translation. This is the commonly accepted explanation and its plausibility is strengthened by the fact that another letter written by Mary to Bothwell about this time has survived in its original French form.

Some obscurities in the text can most easily be explained by assuming a French original. Thus Mary's 'ie' (je), written at speed, may have looked very like 'il'; it became in translation 'he', where 'I' makes better sense. Discrepancies between the Scots and English versions support the theory of a letter in French from which both were derived. Where the Scots says 'to subscrive the same', the English reads 'to have him let blood'. The English translator had read 'signer' as 'saigner'. Certainly it becomes apparent that the English version was not taken from the Scots.

Where the Scots is 'I have drawn it all out of him', the English is 'I have taken the worms out of his nose' which is an ugly literal translation of the French idiom 'tirer les vers du nez' which, incidentally, Mary used in a letter written more than a year later when she was a prisoner in England.

It seems, too, that the letter, as it was poured on to the paper those nights in Glasgow, was not simply the work of one writing in French but of one who had a special familiarity with contemporary French literature. 'And if I had not a proof of his heart of wax,' says the writer, 'And that mine were not of a diamond whereunto no shot can make breach . . .'

> '*Depuis le jour que la première flèche*
> *De ton bel œil m'avança la douleur,*
> *Et que sa blanche et sa noire couleur,*
> *Forçant ma force, au cœur me firent brèche.*'

The quatrain comes from the *Amours* of Ronsard. And Ronsard was the favourite poet of Mary Stuart.

The literary evidence afforded by the letter points all in one direction. But testimony of a different kind is available.

Either the letter is genuine or the author of it has been able to throw himself to a truly extraordinary extent into the character of Mary and the situation in which she found herself. He has invented a whole series of episodes, which were entirely superfluous to his purpose, assuming that he meant to present Mary as a conspirator against her husband's life. For example, there was the incident at Callendar when Lord Livingstone hinted broadly at Bothwell's passion for the Queen. As an invention inserted to give verisimilitude to the story it was bold and dangerous. For Lord Livingstone, a friend of Mary's, would certainly have denied it when the letter was exhibited. He is not known to have done so.

The meetings outside Glasgow with Crawford and later with Hamilton and others might have been widely known at the time. The details of Lennox's health might have been supplied later on to a forger by the Earl himself. But the puzzling remarks about 'the inquisition of Hiegate' and the information given by the laird of Minto to one Walker—these, as they stand, convey nothing to the reader. Why, then, should a forger include in his narrative anything that would merely distract attention from his purpose, the attack on Mary's reputation?

On the other hand, the references concentrate on what would be news to Bothwell while ignoring matters that he would already know. The remarks are, in fact, the completion of a story. The remainder must be sought elsewhere.

The day before she left for Glasgow, Mary wrote in Scots to her ambassador in Paris, the Archbishop of Glasgow, telling him of the reports spread by Hiegate, Minto and Walker, who was a servant of the Archbishop's, that Darnley planned to arrest the Queen and that, contrariwise, some nobles had urged the Queen to arrest Darnley. The person to whom Casket Letter II was addressed was assumed to know of these events. This could only be if the reader in the letter-writer's mind were Bothwell, or a man who had been, like Bothwell, in the Queen's confidence.

There is yet another problem to be faced at this point.

In December 1568, that is, twenty-one months after Mary's arrival in Glasgow, Lennox's retainer, Thomas Crawford, who had met her in the approaches to the town, produced a document which he swore he had written at the time of the visit. It was, on the face of it, an account of his meeting with the Queen and of Darnley's conversations with his wife, based on Darnley's own statement. The report, 1250 words long, corresponds closely at many points with the narrative in Letter II. At some places it corresponds too closely. One passage, about 300 words long, is reproduced almost word for work in the Letter and in Crawford's account.[1]

There are several possible explanations which have been ardently and exhaustively debated by partisan historians:

1. One document simply confirms the other. Writing immediately after the event, Mary and Darnley—by dictation to Crawford—produced two coincident accounts of one of the conversations between husband and wife. It may even be that Darnley posted an eavesdropper to overhear the interview and make notes of it. In the circumstances, this would appear a reasonable precaution on his part. Perhaps Crawford was the hidden listener.

2. Forgers, acting on behalf of Mary's traducers to concoct the Letter in a form damaging to the Queen, made use of Crawford's report, either to tamper with an existing letter of Mary's or to invent a false one.

3. Crawford wrote down, as he claimed he did, what Darnley told him at the time—and later improved on this version by referring to the Letter, which had by that time become available to the Scottish Privy Council.

The first conjecture puts a strain on credulity. It asks us to believe that there could be a similarity, amounting at times to identity, between two separate accounts of the same conversation. Not only have Mary and Darnley (or Crawford) reported the same remarks

1. See Appendix A.

but they have done so in the same phrases. Where there was a possible choice between words they have generally made the same choice.

This would be extraordinary, especially when it is remembered that the Letter, as it has survived, is in the form of a translation from a French original. Darnley reports in English (or Scots) to Crawford, who writes in English. Mary writes in French and is translated. Yet Crawford's version and Mary's are, over considerable stretches, substantially the same!

As for the theory that forgers used Crawford's report to give colour to their work, it is hard to see why they should have done so. For in the portion that is common to both documents there is nothing particularly damaging to Mary. Both report a conversation between two estranged and mutually suspicious persons who, on the surface at least, are warily considering a reconciliation. The Letter injured Mary's character where it reveals her intimacy with Bothwell and the torments of conscience which she is suffering. Of all that there is, of course, nothing in Crawford's story.

Why should counterfeiters have troubled to fabricate an insertion in their work which did not, in fact, improve it from their point of view? Why should they have taken the risk? The Letter would be inspected by sharp eyes. A spurious insertion in an otherwise genuine document would, twice over, risk detection.

To the third possibility there is, obviously, an objection. Although Crawford, preparing his report, might be glad of an opportunity to check it against the Letter, it would be foolish of him to produce an exact copy of the Letter. Perhaps he was carried away by enthusiasm for his task and failed to realise that a near-reproduction of the Letter might actually cast doubts on the authenticity of his story.

When every allowance is made for the perplexities of the problem, the third of the three explanations seems, on balance, the most probable.

On this view both documents, Letter and Report, would be basically authentic.

The conclusion seems inescapable: the second Casket Letter was written by Mary Stuart in the circumstances it describes so minutely and so convincingly.[1] It is not a piece of false evidence concocted to destroy her by painting the picture of a woman bent on crime. It is

1. See also Appendix B.

a self-portrait of one who had committed herself to a purpose from which she shrank and to which she was drawn, reluctantly and in self-hatred, by her over-mastering passion for Bothwell. If at any time her lover had offered her the narrowest way of escape, the slightest encouragement to change her mind, she would have taken it: 'I do here a work that I hate much.'

How subtle, too, is the portrait of Darnley! No monster of wickedness, to be sure, but a man weak and wilful, with the debility of the invalid added to his natural feebleness, with spurts of flickering spirit and passages of ingratiating cajolery which almost win the Queen's conviction. But not quite. In this long blond youth, there is no solid rock of worth or character.

The letter is a marvellously sinister conversation-piece of two deceitful people. In that sick-room in Glasgow the man in bed, horribly marked by his illness, and the dazzling young woman sitting at the bed foot were well matched in distrust and duplicity, although not in intelligence. One has the impression of two wary and dangerous beasts encircling one another in the manœuvres that come before the pounce.

It was Darnley's misfortune that, through a renewal of his physical passion for Mary, he allowed his guard to drop, to the point at least where, although still distrustful, he agreed to go back with her to Edinburgh.

The Second Letter supplies a rational, completely convincing explanation of something that is known to have happened: Darnley's return from Glasgow, where he was comparatively safe, to Edinburgh where he was at the mercy of his enemies. The truly puzzling circumstance about the Letter is, indeed, not that its authenticity has been hard to establish, but that it has been questioned.

For that the blame must be placed upon the poisoned atmosphere of the religious struggle, in which the blindest credulity and the most perverse disbelief could flourish luxuriantly, above all when they were centred on a key personage in the drama, and that personage a queen, beautiful, threatened and, finally, tragic. Loyalty to an embattled Faith: chivalry for a woman; dislike of her more cunning and powerful rival; contempt for the whole squalid pack of nobles, skulking round her throne like jackals; patriotism— all these not unworthy emotions, have conspired through the centuries to prevent the authenticity of the Letter from being accepted.

Even today it is argued that, at most, its credibility depends on circumstantial evidence. This is surely not so. It depends on the application of reasonable canons of probability.

It has been supposed that the Queen wrote another, shorter letter from Glasgow to Bothwell (Casket Letter I). In it she complained that Bothwell seemed to have forgotten her. Waiting for news from him had given her almost as much joy as she would have from his promised answer, when it arrived. In the meantime, she reported 'the man' gay and amorous: 'Summa, you will say, he makes love to me.' 'The man' has been thought to be Darnley whose advances Mary says that she evaded, pleading the pain she had in her side, for which her servant Paris[1] would, she hoped, bring her medicine. When she had brought 'the man' to Craigmillar—if that should be Bothwell's instructions to her—she would go to Edinburgh to be bled.

The letter is dated 'Glasgow, this Saturday, in the morning'. But this is probably a later addition by some clerk. It has been thought, therefore, that the letter was written to Bothwell by Mary on some different occasion. Plausibly enough, it has been argued that 'the man' is Mary's pleasant way of referring to her baby son, whose affection for her gives her so much pleasure that it brings on the pain in her side to which she is subject.

This interpretation of the letter[2] seems as reasonable as the accepted reading. In either case, the Letter, whenever written and from whatever address, adds nothing significant to the story.

Three days after writing Letter II, the Queen left Glasgow to return to Edinburgh, accompanied by her convalescent husband who wore a taffeta mask to hide from the curious the marks of his infection. The macabre little party reached Lord Livingstone's house at Callendar that night. Still no final decision had been taken about where Darnley should stay on his arrival in Edinburgh. Craigmillar Castle was thought of. Bothwell, on the suggestion of

1. Nicholas Hubert, a valet known as French Paris who had formerly been a servant of Bothwell's. Paris had carried the previous letter to Edinburgh.

2. Argued at length by M. H. Armstrong Davison in his study *The Casket Letters*.

Sir James Balfour, favoured a house at Kirk o' Field, just inside the Town Wall of Edinburgh.

Balfour, known in history as Blasphemous Balfour, had already enjoyed a remarkable career; one still more picturesque lay ahead of him. He had been a Protestant and a Catholic, an ecclesiastical lawyer, a parson by trade and a judge by profession. He had rowed in the same French galley as John Knox who reported of his fellow-prisoner, 'He has neither fear of God nor love of virtue'. For once, the Reformer's criticism was, if anything, too gentle.

The idea of using Kirk o' Field no doubt occurred to Balfour because the property belonged to his brother Robert and was standing empty.

In using either this house or Craigmillar the Queen's chief motive was to keep her husband from Holyrood where he might infect the baby prince. By the time the royal couple reached Edinburgh on January 31, the decision in favour of Kirk o' Field had been taken.

It was a group of buildings standing round a courtyard and surrounded by agreeable gardens. It was somewhat remote from the main built up area of the city, and just inside the southern range of the Town Wall. Once the houses had been in ecclesiastical occupation. There were a Provost's House, Prebends' lodgings, a ruined church. In fact, no part of the structure was in good repair.

Darnley was assigned rooms in the Provost's House nearest the Wall. It had already some furniture in it—tapestries, a bed with black velvet hangings and gold and silver fringes, which had been brought from Holyrood for the use of Queen Elizabeth's representative on his way to the christening at Stirling. Darnley did not much care for this bed, but it was a few days before his favourite violet bed, a present from his wife, could be brought out of store.

Immediately below the King's bedroom was an apartment of similar size with a green and yellow bed. Here Mary slept on the nights of February 5 and 7, at Darnley's pleading. Her time was divided between Kirk o' Field and the Palace.

Walking, the distance between the two houses could be covered in about twenty-five minutes. From the Palace it was uphill, through the Canongate village until the High Street of Edinburgh was reached by the Netherbow Port, a gate that was shut at night. Two hundred yards farther on, the route turned sharply to the south, plunging down Blackfriars' Wynd to the Cowgate, a street running parallel to the High Street and at a level about seventy or eighty feet below it. After crossing this thoroughfare, the traveller began the climb to Kirk o' Field, a hundred yards further on.

There were several features about Darnley's lodging which may well have seemed ominous to him. The nearest building of any consequence, a stone's throw distant, was known as the Duke's house. It was the Edinburgh headquarters of the Hamilton family, who had Parliamentary recognition for their claim to the Scottish throne should the line of Stuart die out. The Hamiltons were, for sufficient reason, deadly enemies of the Lennoxes, of whom Darnley's father was head.

A little further off, in St. Mary's Wynd, was Douglas House, town mansion of the great Lowland family ruled by the Earl of Morton, a nobleman whose sole characteristic contribution to human knowledge is the invention of an early version of the guillotine. In due course, Morton sampled his own creation. In the early days of 1567, Darnley can hardly have doubted that Morton bore him a deadly grudge for having betrayed the Riccio murderers to the Queen.

Thus, in quitting Glasgow, Darnley had left the protection of his family's feudal retainers for a neighbourhood that was, to say the least, unfriendly. He had done so by gambling on his wife's renewed good will.

7 'On Sunday, we'll do it'

Edinburgh was a capital given to wild feeling, bitterness, suspicion; apprehensions were endemic to the place, carried on the winds that search through its closes. In those early February days, the atmosphere was high-pitched and nervous.

A clash was at hand, perhaps between Town and Palace, Calvin and Rome, today and yesterday. Something at any rate was afoot, violent but different from the aimless butcheries of the past, the exhausted feuds. What exactly, no one knew. Who was threatened? One raised an eyebrow, nodded, in a certain direction. Prudent people thought of making a visit to the country. One or two, most likely to be embroiled, vanished from the streets. It was some time since Edinburgh had been comforted by the voice of John Knox. As far away as London and Paris, rumours were heard.

Mary's ambassador at the French Court, the Archbishop of Glasgow, had picked up reports at once so sinister and so vague that he committed them to cypher and, at the time the Queen was still in Glasgow, sent them to Edinburgh by one of the Scottish Archers, Robert Drury. His letter told the Queen to take heed. He had heard from the Spanish ambassador that some surprise against her was to be attempted in Scotland. What its nature was he could not discover although he had carried his enquiries as high as the ear of Catherine de' Medici herself. She pooh-poohed the whole thing.

The Archbishop would not be at ease until he heard from Mary again.

The story he had picked up was prevalent in Spanish circles at the time. It reached the Duchess of Parma in the Netherlands and the Spanish ambassador in London. Probably it referred to the plot against Mary in which Darnley was involved at the time of the

75

christening of their son. In that case, the danger to Mary was over before the Archbishop put pen to paper. The chief actor in the supposed conspiracy had fallen under the Queen's spell and become her captive.

While the Archbishop's warning was still on its way to Mary, Sir William Cecil heard from the English agent in Edinburgh of a curious and equivocal episode there. Mary's half-brother, Lord Robert Stewart, had tipped off Darnley that he was about to be assassinated. Darnley, true to his reputation as one who could not keep a secret, passed the titbit on to Mary who had brought the two quick-tempered young men face to face. Each laid a hand on his sword. In haste, Mary summoned the Earl of Moray to the room; a duel was averted.

The Queen's enemies have interpreted this incident as an attempt by Mary to promote a scuffle in which her husband might be killed. A letter of hers to Bothwell, which may belong to the time, has been held to confirm this. The letter is, in fact, so obscure in its terms that it can hardly be regarded as evidence for anything. And by calling Moray to the scene Mary effectively clears herself from the suspicion of having sought to become a widow by so elegant a stratagem. However, the story has some importance since it shows that by February 8, when Cecil recorded it, the early removal of Darnley was expected by the well-informed English Government.

So far as the Scottish Queen was concerned, she seemed to be busy with more domestic matters. One of her maids had become pregnant. Given the severe attitude to sexual lapses which the Calvinist revolution had introduced, this might be most embarrassing. Four years earlier, the Queen's apothecary and one of her servants had been hanged for abortion, thus providing the theme for a famous ballad, 'The Queen's Maries'.[1]

Now it seemed that the scandal might be repeated, with all the odium which would be roused in a censorious town like Edinburgh. There, only three months before, the council had decreed that anyone who allowed a harlot to make use of his house should be fined £10 for the first offence. It is possible that the letter in which Mary mentions this tiresome business refers to her own *femme de chambre* Margaret Carwood. If that is so, then Mary in the end

1. The four Maries were maids of honour and at no time was any of them involved in so squalid an affair.

decided not only to forgive the offender but to give her the royal blessing.

Margaret was to marry John Stewart of Tullypowreis, a few days after the marriage of Christina Hogg to Bastien Pages, one of the Queen's valets, an Auvergnat, light-hearted and musical, a favourite with the Court. As the Lord Treasurer's Accounts for 1567 show, Mary gave her valet and her waiting woman black satin and velvet for dresses to the value of 183 pounds Scots.[1]

Meanwhile, the exact means by which Darnley was to be removed were settled, by Bothwell and his closest associates, Sir James Balfour and Archibald Douglas, a member of the great house and, beyond all question, one of the most accomplished villains in Scotland. Truly, a formidable claim, yet one that could be made with some confidence for this Douglas. How well he and Balfour were matched, each an assassin, each a traitor and each—in his own peculiar way—an ecclesiastic! Douglas became minister of Glasgow Cathedral; soon afterwards he arranged for the murder of his cousin the Earl of Morton but 'the gun made no service'.

After deep cogitation, Bothwell, who had apparently been at first in favour of killing Darnley 'in the fields', perhaps outside the Town Wall, changed his mind. He gave his decision for gunpowder which, at some convenient moment, would be exploded in the room below Darnley's.

This was on Friday, the 7th of February. Time was running short. Very soon, Darnley's convalescence would be over. He would have taken the final cleansing bath which marked his return to health and he would certainly expect his wife to resume marital relations as she had promised. The prospect filled Mary with horror. She detested the man and, possibly, feared that he suffered from a continuing infection.

As for Bothwell, he was jealous by nature and violent by habit. Now that he had the Queen's love—and who will doubt that he had it, in the full, physical sense! we are dealing with a race, a time and a caste in which blood ran hot and quickly—was it likely that he would tolerate the disowned, despised and hated husband resuming his rights?

Casket Letter II shows Mary, with the instinctive art of a woman

1. In English money of the time this would represent about £45.

in her situation, half-teasing her lover's passion, half-soothing his jealousy. If her deceptive love-play with Darnley, in which there may have been a tincture of sincerity (or, at least, regret), had ever turned into surrender to his passion, then it is likely the sequel would have been short and brutal. Either Mary or Darnley—and perhaps both of them—would have been strangled by her lover.

What Mary knew about Bothwell's intentions on February 8 can only be guessed. Certainly she knew that he meant to rid her of her husband. That was why she had gone, not without danger, to Glasgow and persuaded Darnley, not without art, to return with her to Edinburgh. But the machinery of the plot, the exact nature of what was planned—it is likely that Mary knew as little about that as anyone in Holyroodhouse who was outside the circle of the conspiracy. Morton knew; Lethington knew; Bothwell knew, of course; Moray probably guessed—but Mary both knew and did not know—a privilege of princes.

When Bothwell decided in favour of gunpowder, the powder, it seems, was already in the lower hall of his quarters in the Palace. At that time, Holyrood was larger, more confused and infinitely more picturesque than the tame Renaissance palace that now exists. Bothwell's quarters were, it seems, on the south side facing the garden, on two floors connected by a turnpike stair in the Scottish fashion. The powder, brought from Dunbar Castle, a royal fortress under Bothwell's control, seems to have lain there for three days.

This was only one of the risks run by Bothwell at this time. It was not the most hazardous.

Having decided how the task was to be accomplished, he had still to choose the team of his assistants.

It was not a task that presented any great difficulty. Scotland had no shortage of cut-throats just then. And after all, he was at that moment the most powerful man in the country, and the enterprise to which he was setting his hand had the moral support of important persons in the nobility. Huntly knew what was afoot, so did Morton and Argyll. Lethington, the Secretary of State, was well aware that some decisive and probably bloody business was at hand of which Darnley, the Queen's husband and titular King, was the designated victim.

Moray, eldest half-brother of the Queen, was in a somewhat different position. He knew that Mary wanted to be free of her husband. He can hardly have doubted, looking at the men who had his sister's ear, that desperate methods might be used. But he kept himself strictly aloof. He was well cast for the frustrating role of royal bastard, conscious that he had inherited the gift of rule along with a veto on its use in the highest place. He was a Protestant, serious and severe as his father had been loose, torn between love and hatred for his sister, between a brother's impulse to protect her on the throne and a statesman's ambition to save the state. Between those two, sister and brother, there was a bond other than the tie of blood, in which hatred—and therefore affection?—jealousy—and therefore love?—played their part.

Mary is said to have egged on her husband Darnley, at a time when she no longer loved him, to seduce Moray's wife. The report lacks confirmation yet somehow trails the odour of truth. When Moray was, in the end, murdered, his sister, out of her private income, gave the assassin a pension.

After Darnley's death and her disastrous marriage to Bothwell, the Queen was a prisoner in the keeping of Moray's mother. Moray visited her. The violence with which he upbraided her then —what did it spring from? Anger at her madness in throwing away the crown? Outraged morality, which he at least in Scotland could indulge without hypocrisy? Or was there, in the brutality of his denunciation, a streak of deeper resentment?

During the days immediately before the death of Darnley the Earl of Moray, knowing something and guessing more of what was being prepared, took no step to prevent the destruction of a man whom, certainly, he despised.

Bothwell could go forward with his recruitment of assistants knowing that some warmly approved and nobody overtly opposed. He sought men who belonged to one or other of two kinds—the executants and the workmen—and his search for them did not reach outside a comparatively narrow circle of men on whom he could rely, for one reason or another: a few Border lairds, dependants of his family and himself, and a few personal servants. The first type were men of his own kind, bold and careless of the niceties of law; the second were capable of obeying a simple order and unaccustomed to question one when it was given.

The executants were John Hay the younger, of Tala, James Ormiston of Ormiston, who lived in the Moss Tower in Teviotdale, his uncle Robert Ormiston, and John Hepburn of Bowton, a cousin of Bothwell's. The workmen were William Powrie, George Dalgleish, Bothwell's valet Pat Wilson, who seems to have been a labourer in his service, and a Frenchman, Nicolas Hubert, known as French Paris.

Paris had once been a servant of Bothwell's; now he was in the Queen's household as a *valet de chambre*. His part in the conspiracy is one of the most important and the evidence which he later gave, in unpleasant cirumstances, establishes him as a clearly marked human type—naive, intelligent, voluble, frightened, and tricky—the petty professional rogue trying to wriggle his way out of a scrape. His memory as a witness and, no doubt, his imagination were powerfully stimulated by a near view of the instruments of torture. Those who listened to his confession or, later on, would read it, had strong motives for editing the narrative if this were necessary. Paris's instinctive desire would be to save them this trouble if he could do so.

With this caution in mind, his account of the events leading up to the night of February 9–10 may be read. By reason of its primacy in the sequence of events, the contribution of Paris justly opens what may be called The Murderer's Tale.

He had been in the Queen's retinue on her journey to Glasgow. At Callendar, Mary had handed him a purse containing three or four hundred crowns, telling him to carry it to Lord Bothwell. When he took the purse from Paris, Bothwell said, 'If you take care what you are doing, the Queen will give you letters to bring to me.' And so it turned out.

Two days after she arrived in Glasgow, Mary gave the valet letters to deliver to Bothwell and Lethington in Edinburgh. At the same time, she instructed Paris to keep a sharp eye on the two men as they talked and watch the expressions on their faces. It was a question, she explained, of deciding whether the air at Craigmillar or Kirk o' Field would be more beneficial for the King in his convalescence.

When Paris reached Edinburgh, he found that Lord Bothwell was dining tête-à-tête with that eminent jurist, Sir James Balfour. The Earl read the letter and, in Balfour's presence, wrote a reply. 'Tell the Queen,' he said to the valet, 'that everything will go well. Tell her I send her this diamond and, if I had my heart, I would send it.

Go to Lethington,' he added, 'and ask him if he wishes to write to the Queen.' Thereupon, Paris sought out the Secretary of State at the Exchequer, a building near St. Giles' Church. Having weighed the matter up, Lethington gave his opinion: the King would be better off at Kirk o' Field. Paris made his way back to Glasgow with the two messages.

Mary cross-examined him closely about the interviews. She told Paris that it was her intention to appoint Gilbert Curle *valet de chambre* to the King in place of Sandy Durham, whom she did not trust. Although this change was, in fact, never made, the incident shows that the Queen was, at this time, closely supervising the details of her husband's household.

Paris accompanied the Queen and Darnley on their journey back to Edinburgh. From Linlithgow Palace, where they spent a night, he was dispatched by Mary on another errand, this time to carry bracelets to Bothwell—the bracelets which are mentioned in Casket Letter II.

So far as Paris's memory served him, the next event with any bearing on the matter occurred on Wednesday or perhaps Thursday, February 5 or 6, at a time when the Queen was staying in her little bedroom under Darnley at Kirk o' Field. Paris, on duty after dinner in the room, was approached by Bothwell who whispered in his ear, 'Paris, I am ill with my usual sickness.[1] Don't you know a place where I could go?' '*Ma foi*,' replied the valet, 'I was never here until today, but I will go and find a place.'

Between two doors, Paris found a suitable place: 'Come here if you are pressed.' He helped Bothwell to take off his clothes.

In this secluded place a strange dialogue between the two men occurred. 'How are you?' asked Bothwell. 'Very well,' said Paris, 'thanks to God and your lordship'—having been rewarded for any service he had done the Earl by being appointed one of the *valets de chambre* to the Queen. 'It is not enough,' said Bothwell. 'You covered my dishonour when you were in my service abroad.'

This may be a reference to Bothwell's alleged addiction to unnatural vice or to his reputation as a practitioner of witchcraft. 'I knew his very terrible vices,' said Paris in another part of his story, 'especially one in which I am said to be so good a minister. I told him more than six years ago, it would be his ruin.'

1. Bothwell was troubled with dysentery.

The widespread belief that Bothwell was addicted to homo-
sexual practices depends chiefly on the evidence of an ex-servant of
his, Dandie Pringle, whom he had dismissed for trying to poison
him. Pringle uttered horrifying stories of his ex-master in ears that
were only too ready to believe him, those of the Earl of Bedford,
Queen Elizabeth's Governor of Berwick, who lost no time in
passing them on to Cecil: 'as naughty a man as liveth and much
given to that vile and detestable vice of sodomy'.

Whatever be the meaning of Bothwell's ingratiating remarks, he
plunged forthwith into more momentous business: 'If the King has
ever the advantage over us other lords, he will want to dominate us
and we do not mean to put up with it; we mean to blow him up in
this house with gunpowder. What do you think of that?'

'You will pardon me if I don't tell you.'

'What are you saying? Do you want to preach at me?'

'No, you misunderstand me. For the five or six years that I was
in your lordship's service, I have often seen you in great trouble and
I never saw any friends who helped you then. Now you are out of
those troubles. Everybody, great or small, pays you court. But—I
don't know—you are of the country, my lord. They say you are
now the greatest landowner in it and also you are married. That is
usually the time when a young man decides to stop . . . And now
you propose to undertake this big enterprise, far bigger than any
trouble you have ever had, for everyone will cry *"ho harault!"*[1]
on you.'

Bothwell: 'Are you stupid enough to think that I am doing this
alone? I have with me Lethington who is considered to have one of
the best minds in this country. He is the presiding genius of it all.
I have Argyll, my brother-in-law Huntly, Morton, Ruthven and
Lindsay. I have the signatures of those men, written the last time we
were at Craigmillar.'

Paris: 'You have not named Moray, loved by the common
people.'[2]

1. French hunting term equivalent to 'raise the hue and cry'.

2. This part of Paris's narrative arouses suspicion. His account was given
in August 1569, two and a half years after the events he is describing, and at a
time when Moray was Regent of Scotland. It seems more likely that Paris
actually uttered the words to flatter the ruler (vainly as it turned out) than
that they were inserted in his statement by another hand. Moray had no need
of flatterers at that time.

Bothwell: 'He will take no part in it.'

He then told the valet to take possession of the key of the Queen's room at Kirk o' Field. Paris objected: the usher would ask him what he meant to do with it.

Bothwell: 'Aren't you the Queen's valet?'

Paris: 'But it is the usher's duty to look after the key.'

At that Bothwell left; Paris picked up his cloak and sword and walked thoughtfully to St. Giles', the chief church in the town. During his meditations, he came to the conclusion that it was useless for him to think of escaping to England where he would certainly be arrested for lack of a passport. Whatever misgivings he might have about the way matters were developing, he had no alternative but to stay in Edinburgh.

That was, at any rate, how Paris recalled the working of his mind all these months later, when his fears were powerfully reinforced by the ugly turn events had taken. Meanwhile Bothwell had brought a supply of gunpowder to Holyroodhouse from Dunbar Castle, a royal arsenal of which he was governor. Next day, probably February 6, Bothwell broached the business to his cousin-german John Hepburn of Bowton—in language which did not lack plainness. 'Some of the nobles,' he said, 'I among them, propose that the King should be slain and that everyone of us should send two of his servants to do it. Will you be one?'

Hepburn, according to his own recollection, at first objected. He found the proposal a thoroughly bad one. But, in the end, as a relation and retainer of Bothwell's, he succumbed to his cousin's arguments: he agreed to do what the others would do. At that time, Bothwell seems to have had no fixed idea about how the murder should be carried out.

John Hay, younger, of Tala had been one of the attendants on the Queen during her journey to Glasgow. On the return journey, while they were at Linlithgow Palace, Mary had spoken at some length to him. After this audience, Tala rode off to see Bothwell in Edinburgh, carrying some private message. But it seems that the first Tala heard of the conspiracy against the King's life was on Friday, February 7, in Bothwell's lodging in Holyrood.

Having sworn the young Laird to secrecy, Bothwell came to the point with his usual abruptness. He said he meant to kill Darnley: 'If I don't put him down I can't have any sort of life in

Scotland.' From that moment Tala was a party to the enterprise.

On the same day, Bothwell sent for Paris and asked him if he had the key to the Queen's chamber at Kirk o' Field. When Paris replied that he meant to get it, Bothwell said sharply, 'Don't fail. On Sunday, we'll do it!' The Frenchman, according to his own account, suffered one of his fits of prudence or bad conscience. He set off for Leith meaning to find there a ship to flee in. But what was the good? he reflected. How could he, a mere valet, charter a ship? It was ridiculous. He went sombrely back to the Palace.

There Bothwell spent some time in drawing his bailiff Ormiston of that Ilk, known as 'Black' Ormiston, into the plot. Ormiston's first inclination was to refuse. Bothwell pressed him. 'You need fear nothing. All the lords have come to the same conclusion.' Black Ormiston succumbed to this argument.

That evening in the presence of Hepburn, Ormiston and Tala, Bothwell explained the project in fuller detail. The gunpowder would be laid in the room under the King's bedroom—that is, the room the Queen slept in when she stayed at Kirk o' Field—in a barrel, with a hole at the lower end, through which a trough-shaped piece of wood with a lint in it would be inserted. Originally it had been planned to carry out the murder on Saturday night, but preparations could not be completed in time—perhaps it was a question of Paris's failure to get the key—and the business was postponed.

After the conference, Ormiston returned to his Edinburgh lodging in Blackfriars' Wynd, at the house of Thomas Henderson, better known in the town as Katy's Tam, owing to the fact that his mother's name was Kate. There, Ormiston spent the whole of the next day (Saturday) in bed. Bothwell was not so idle.

Mary dined that night with her husband at Kirk o' Field. Bothwell was one of the company. After dinner, he again demanded the key of the Queen's chamber from Paris and, without giving the valet time to answer, told him that he had already enough keys without any help from him; he taunted Paris with his lack of courage. Paris at once went into the Queen's chamber where he found Margaret Carwood and others of the Queen's attendants waiting for her grace to come down from Darnley's room overhead.

The report ran round from mouth to mouth and room to room

that the Queen was leaving for Holyrood at once. The Queen's people scurried out of the bedchamber. Paris was last to leave. The key was in the door. He slipped it out, concealed it and produced it in triumph to Bothwell. 'Keep it,' said the nobleman. Opening a little coffer, he showed Paris a number of keys all freshly counterfeited, although who the forger was Paris did not know.[1]

An hour later, at the Palace, Margaret Carwood told him to go back to Kirk o' Field and fetch a bedcover from the Queen's room. While he was on this errand, Darnley's *valet de chambre*, Sandy Durham, asked him for the key. 'It is for the usher to give it to you,' said Paris. He returned to the Palace and handed the bedcover over to Mrs. Carwood.

1. Paris gave two versions of this incident assigning it in one to Friday and in another to Saturday. A great deal has been made of such discrepancies in Paris's story. But they seem to reflect on the incompetence of his interrogators rather than on his veracity. After two years and more, it was not surprising that his recollection of dates was confused.

8   The murderers' tale

NEXT DAY (FEBRUARY 9) the last Sunday before Lent was, by tradition, a day of carnival in Edinburgh, when every form of frivolity might be expected, even under the disapproving eyes of the new Church.

Paris, who rose at six o'clock, was the first of the conspirators abroad. After a stroll in the Queen's park, he breakfasted with three of her officers and, at nine, was on duty in the Palace. There he found the Earl of Moray taking leave of his sister. Apparently, his lordship had been on his way to the sermon when word reached him that his wife, at St. Andrews, was expecting a child. Moray proposed to ride, with all possible speed, to her bedside.

After playing his part in the ceremonial of departure, Paris, who was of a restless disposition, and had many disagreeable matters on his mind, walked to the village of Restalrig, a mile or so away. He returned to the Palace to find that the Queen was making ready to take part in the dinner which was part of the festivities for the wedding of her valet, Bastien Pages.

At four o'clock that afternoon there was a meeting in the lower hall of Bothwell's lodging in the Palace. Present were James Ormiston, his uncle Rob (Robert) Ormiston and Hay of Tala. Aware of the gathering, but knowing nothing of what was discussed, was a porter of Bothwell's, William Powrie who, on the previous day, had at his master's behest obtained a half-fathom of lint from one of the soldiers of the guard whose name he did not know. He passed the lint to Hepburn. Before Sunday was over, Powrie was amply acquainted with the practical outcome of the talk.

As Tala remembered later on, the conspirators arranged before they left that, as soon as it was dark, they should make their way to the Laird of Ormiston's lodging in Blackfriars' Wynd. As dusk was falling, John Hepburn sent Tala's servant to fetch an empty powder-barrel from a man dwelling above Sandy Bruce's closehead[1] on the north side of High Street.

In the meantime, Mary attended by a company of nobles, the Earls of Huntly, Argyll, Cassillis and Bothwell, had gone to a fare-well supper given by the Bishop of Argyll to the departing Savoyard envoy, Robertino Solaro di Moretta, remembered as the man in whose train David Riccio had first come to Scotland. Since the supper party was held in Sir James Balfour's house in Blackfriars' Wynd, borrowed for the occasion, it can only have been a short distance from Ormiston's apartment in the same street.

At supper, Paris performed his duties as valet, presenting the basin and towel to his mistress after the meal. She asked him, 'Have you taken the bedcovering from the King's lodging?' Paris said he had done so. A great deal has been made of this incident as if the Queen, knowing what was about to happen at Kirk o' Field, had made sure of saving one of her possessions from destruc-tion.

This seems a far-fetched deduction. Mary's was not the kind of temperament that concerned itself with small matters of property when great and enthralling issues were at stake. She was leaving in Kirk o' Field valuable tapestries and furnishings from the royal stores. Why, then, should she worry about a bed covering? If any-thing, Mary's remark to Paris would seem to indicate that she did not know what Bothwell's plan was.

At length the nobles—Huntly, Argyll and the rest—rose from the dinner table and took leave of their host and the ambassador. Bothwell beckoned to Paris to follow him. While the others made their way to Kirk o' Field with the Queen, the Earl and the valet called at the house nearby occupied by Bothwell's mother, the Lady of Morham, and, after a few minutes, went to Ormiston's lodging where they found the Black Laird and his uncle Rob.

Such is the account of events given later by Paris; but it seems that Bothwell paid another visit to Ormiston that evening, perhaps before he went to the Bishop of Argyll's supper party. The Laird of Tala says that he accompanied Bothwell and John Hepburn to

1. i.e. the entrance to the close from the street.

Ormiston's lodging where, at the foot of the stair, they found a man named Ade Murray and some others. These Bothwell sent about their business. Upstairs were Ormiston, his uncle and a brother, who was promptly put to the door. Intruders were not welcome at that moment.

As Ormiston remembered the events of the evening, he remained in his room until Hepburn and Tala entered to tell him that the Queen and the lords had left the Bishop's supper party and were on their way to visit the King. Bothwell, they said, was waiting at the crossing of Blackfriars' Wynd and the Cowgate. On hearing this news, Ormiston threw on a riding cloak and went out into the cold. After some searching in the streets, he met Bothwell who had, in the meantime, fallen in with Rob Ormiston.

The conspirators discussed by which route the gunpowder could most conveniently be brought into Kirk o' Field. After some argument they walked together down the Wynd to the gate leading into Blackfriars' Church. Through some tumbledown old houses, Ormiston entered the grounds and opened the gate to the others from the inside.

The approach to Kirk o' Field through Blackfriars had obvious advantages. The grounds were bounded on the south by the Town Wall, twenty-one feet high, on the west by a wall abutting on the Kirk o' Field property. It was possible therefore to come within a few yards of Darnley's lodging while remaining unseen by passers-by in the streets. Blackfriars' Gate would serve as a useful rendezvous.

Paris, describing these events, simply says that Bothwell and he, together with the Ormistons, went to the Cowgate where they met Tala and Hepburn. After some discussion in the street, Bothwell and Paris set off for Kirk o' Field. Halfway there, the Earl gave the valet his orders: 'You will go to the Queen's room. When John Hepburn, Tala and Ormiston come in and have done what they want to do, you will go upstairs to the King's room which you will leave by any means you like.'

If Tala's account of this part of the action differs from that of Paris, too much should not be made of the discrepancies. Both men are speaking at some time after the happenings of that night, Tala eleven months later, Paris two and a half years afterwards. The events themselves were compressed, alike in time and space, within about half an hour and 200 yards of Edinburgh streets. It is easy to understand that minor incidents might be forgotten or confused.

Both accounts involve some telescoping of the action. For instance, it is possible that Bothwell, after giving Paris his orders, returned to the Ormistons for a final consultation and arrived at the King's lodgings some time after the valet. Certainly, at some stage, Hepburn must have left the others and made his way to Holyrood, where he had urgent business.

It was about half past nine. In the next few hours there was a great deal to do.

In the meantime, in Kirk o' Field, Darnley, behind his taffeta mask, was entertaining his wife and the nobles she had brought with her. The scene did not lack colour and animation: nobles and ladies in their handsomest clothes, candles glimmering on the Coney-catcher tapestry brought from the store at Holyrood, chatter and laughter, dicing at a table covered with green velvet, Mary in a high chair upholstered in violet beside her husband's bed.

She talked—as the others diced—in the most carefree manner in the world. It was about midnight before she said she must leave. Had she not promised to dance at Bastien's wedding in the Palace? Her husband expostulated. She had agreed, he reminded her, that she would spend the night in the room below. Mary replied that next day he would be out of quarantine; they could sleep together at the Palace.

While this revelry was going on in the King's lodging, activities of quite a different kind were taking place at Holyroodhouse, known familiarly as 'the Abbey' from its earlier monastic associations.

About ten o'clock that night, Bothwell's porter William Powrie, was ordered by John Hepburn to move two portmanteaux, one of wood, the other of leather, which were standing in the lower hall of Bothwell's quarters. Powrie and Pat Wilson were ordered to load the trunks on a grey horse belonging to Bothwell's page Hermon. In this way the trunks were carried through the streets of Edinburgh to the gate leading into the Blackfriars' grounds. There they were emptied of their contents, which consisted of gunpowder in bags of convenient size, called polks.

The night being moonless the work went forward slowly so

that Hepburn sent Powrie to find candles. The porter bought half a dozen from Geordie Bruce's wife in the Cowgate. One of them was lit and, by the light, the two trunks were emptied. Each man carried a polk on his back to the wall which divided the garden of Kirk o' Field from the Blackfriars' grounds. At that point Ormiston, Tala and Hepburn took over the powder. Powrie and Wilson were allowed to go no farther.

As there was still powder left in the Palace, the two servants went back to fetch it and, on the second journey, brought with them in addition the empty powder barrel which, that evening, Tala's servant had fetched from the man who lived above Sandy Bruce's closehead.

On this second trip, Powrie muttered to his companion, 'Jesus, what kind of road is this we are going! I think it's no good.' Wilson apparently shared this doubt but replied, 'Wheesht! Haud your tongue.' Thus at least Powrie remembered the dialogue which was certainly neither improbable nor unjustified.

At the Blackfriars' Gate, Powrie and his companion were met by Rob Ormiston, who was frankly sceptical about prospects. Shaking his head, he said: 'This is not good like. I don't believe this affair will come about tonight. I will go in and see what they are doing.'

When the second load of powder had been set down at the gate, the Laird of Ormiston appeared from the direction of Kirk o' Field, French Paris with him. 'By God,' said the Laird to Hepburn and Tala, 'it is fair in field, come of it what may.' He told Powrie and Pat Wilson to make off back to the Palace.

Sometime during that night, Powrie claims that he saw Bothwell, Rob Ormiston and French Paris at the Blackfriars' Gate. With them were two other men, with cloaks about their faces and slippers on their feet. Apparently then—for there is no reason to doubt Powrie's word on this matter—there was an occasion when Bothwell left the party in Kirk o' Field to see for himself how the preparations were going forward.

Hepburn says that, while they were filling the polks with powder, Bothwell arrived and asked if everything was ready. 'Hurry up,' he said. 'Finish the job before the Queen comes out of the house or you will not find it so convenient.'

After this he went to join the other nobles of the Queen's party.

Paris made his way to the kitchen of Kirk o' Field and asked Bonkil the cook for a candle. This he lit in the Queen's bedroom. By its light Hepburn and Tala brought in the gunpowder in polks and poured it out in a heap on the floor. They had intended to use the barrel to contain the powder and increase the force of the explosion but this was impossible. The barrel was too big to be brought into the room and they left it in the yard outside.

While they were at this work, Bothwell entered in a state of alarm. 'My God!' he said, 'what a noise you are making! Everything you do can be heard upstairs!' Having given the warning, the Earl returned to the King's bedroom, followed in a little by Paris, who, before leaving the room below, locked the door connecting it with the turnpike stair which led up to Darnley's bedchamber.

When he arrived upstairs, Paris made a signal to Bothwell that all was in readiness. So at least Tala reported who, since he was locked in the room below with the gunpowder, cannot have seen the gesture. Lord Argyll patted the valet affectionately on the back without uttering a word. Paris seems to have regarded this gesture as a sign of complicity and, probably, he was right.

The Frenchman had been in the room for no longer than the length of a paternoster when the Queen took her departure. Darnley pressed her to stay, but, good-humouredly, she insisted on going and gave him a fine ring as a pledge that, very soon, they would be together as husband and wife.

When she caught sight of Paris, Mary exclaimed, 'Jesus, how black you are!' This, at any rate, is a story told by the Queen's secretary Claude Nau. It does not seem improbable that Paris, who had been handling gunpowder immediately before, was in a grimy state.

The Queen's little cavalcade, torches burning, made its way down the steep incline towards the Cowgate and then up Blackfriars' Wynd to the High Street. William Powrie and Pat Wilson, carrying the empty trunks back to the Palace—the grey horse had vanished—caught sight of the royal party some distance ahead of them.

Black Ormiston had given the final instructions to Hepburn and Tala: 'Now you know what you have to do. When all is quiet above you, fire the lint and come your way.' Then Ormiston and his uncle made off, the former to bed in his lodging in Katy's Tam's house. This he reached as a church clock struck the hour.[1]

Left in Kirk o' Field, Darnley prepared for the night. He gave orders that his three great horses should be ready, saddled and bridled, at five o'clock. The Queen was about to ride to Seton in the morning. He had the intention of doing the same.

It is possible, however, that Darnley had quite a different purpose in mind. He can hardly have been at ease in his mind about the situation. He can hardly have taken comfort from the company in which he found himself. The dark, fierce visage of Bothwell was scarcely one to inspire confidence.

Even if his wife, the Queen, did not utter that casual reminder—as she is reported to have done during the evening—that it was just eleven months since Riccio was murdered, there were probably other incidents that night likely to make him thoughtful. He may have contemplated making a bolt for it with the first light. Certainly the order for his horses at such an hour seems odd in a young man recovering from a serious illness.

Whatever Darnley's apprehensions may have been, they were not acute enough for him to make a search of the house which would have led to the discovery of a locked room immediately below his bedchamber. Trust in his wife, distrust of her—the conflict between those moods had been resolved by physical weakness in a numb acceptance of fate.

Darnley sang the fifth psalm with one of his servants: 'Lead me, O Lord, in Thy righteousness because of mine enemies; make Thy way straight before my face.' He called for wine and drank a good-night toast. Then he went to bed, his valet William Taylor sleeping in the room with him. Soon all was quiet in Kirk o' Field.

In Bothwell's apartments at Holyrood, Powrie and Wilson waited an hour or more for orders. Meanwhile in the royal apartments, a puzzling episode was being enacted. The Queen, after dancing at Bastien Pages' wedding feast, had a prolonged consultation with Bothwell and John Stewart of Traquair, Captain of the Guard. For her the revels were ended.

What was said at this secret colloquy can only be guessed but, most likely, it related to the events that immediately followed. It

1. Probably eleven.

James Hepburn, Earl of Bothwell

Artist unknown

would be sensible to warn the sentries round the Palace to expect unusual comings and goings during the night. Some pretext for these movements might be given to Traquair, who was probably not privy to the plot.

After the captain left the room, Bothwell and Mary had a brief talk with no witnesses present. Then the Earl joined his servants in his apartment.

He took off the black satin doublet and the velvet hose trimmed with silver that he had been wearing and pulled on black hose without any adornment, a canvas doublet and his riding cloak of English cloth in what was called the 'new colour'.

Noticing that Paris had a woebegone look, Bothwell turned on him furiously. 'Why do you look like that?' and promised the valet a thrashing such as he had never had in his life. Paris replied that he was ill and would like to go to bed. Bothwell would have none of it. 'You'll come with me,' he said to the poor wretch.

Followed by Paris, Powrie, Pat Wilson and Geordie Dalgleish, he ran down the turnpike stair. Outside, in the black February night, he led the way along the back wall of the Queen's garden, heading past the Mint and the rear of the royal stables towards the Canongate. At the gateway between the garden and the outer close of the Palace, two soldiers of the guard were on sentry duty. A shout came out of the darkness, 'Who is that?' 'Friends.' 'What friends?' 'My Lord Bothwell's friends.' On hearing this name, the sentries insisted no further.

The party advanced quietly westward along the Canongate until they saw looming above them the crenellations and the steeple of the Netherbow Port. They had reached the entrance to the city of Edinburgh proper at the moment when the gate was being shut for the night. If John Galloway the gatekeeper was as punctual in his duties as he should have been, it would be about midnight. But it must have been somewhat later.

Pat Wilson called out to Galloway, 'Open to friends of Lord Bothwell's.' Galloway appeared after a reasonable delay and eyed the nightbirds with no great enthusiasm before he opened the gate. 'What are you doing out of your beds at this time of night?' he enquired. He was given no answer. The five men, on their desperate mission, were now within the Town Wall which the burgesses of Edinburgh had built to protect them from English invaders.

They were in streets patrolled every night by thirty-two men of the town watch and subject to the jealous moral surveillance of the elders of St. Giles' High Kirk.

Holding to the south side of the High Street they pressed on, close to the buildings until the house of Bassandyne, the most celebrated Scottish printer of the age. Here, in an apartment above a sword slipper's shop, was where Black Ormiston lived. They knocked. Silence. Then somebody answered, untruthfully as we know, that the Laird was not there.

The five plunged down through a steep close towards the Cowgate which they crossed in order to reach the Blackfriars' Gate where, earlier that night, they had taken the gunpowder out of the trunks.

Telling the others to await his return without stirring, no matter what they saw or heard, Bothwell set off over the wall which divided the Blackfriars property from Kirk o' Field gardens. He took Paris with him. He was gone about half an hour, as they judged, before they heard anything.

By two o'clock, all sounds had died down in Darnley's lodging. Hepburn and Tala, locked in the lower room with the gunpowder, decided that the time had come to act. They put the lint in the little wooden trough with one end in the heap of powder. The other end they lit. Then they made off into the darkness as quietly as possible, locking the doors behind them with the duplicate keys which Bothwell had given them. At the wall between Kirk o' Field and Blackfriars, they came upon the Earl himself, well wrapped in his heavy riding cloak and a prey to extreme nervous excitement.

Bothwell asked if they had done what he told them to do. 'Yes,' they answered. There followed what seemed to all of them—but stretched nerves are bad timekeepers—a long delay. Bothwell became angry and wanted to go back to the house to see what was happening.

'You need not,' Hepburn told him.

'I won't leave until I see it doing,' Bothwell insisted. 'Is there a window through which I can see if the lint is burning?'

'Yes, but only a window on the quadrangle.'

Just at that moment a flash of light appeared in one of the windows of the house. An instant later the building rose in the air

before their eyes. There was a tremendous explosion. They took
to their heels through the Blackfriars' grounds to the Cowgate, and
were seen and accosted as they passed by Mrs. Barbara Martin and
Mrs. Mary Crockett: 'Traitors, you have been at some evil turn!'
They hurried on without answering.

Then they divided into two: one party reaching the High Street
by way of Blackfriars' Wynd, the other taking a parallel route
through an adjacent alley. They reassembled in the Netherbow not
far from the Town Gate. Through an alley which took them farther
north, they reached a section of the Town Wall which they knew
to be in a tumbledown state. However, Bothwell, who had injured
his hand not long before in a fight with a Border robber, decided
that the jump was too high for him.

They returned to the Netherbow Port where Bothwell bade
Hepburn shout to John Galloway to open to friends of Lord
Bothwell's. Rising from his bed, Galloway let them out of the
town. After that, they divided again. Some went down the
Canongate, others reached the Palace through St. Mary's Wynd
and a path leading behind the gardens of the Canongate
houses.

Paris found himself next to Tala who said gloomily, 'We have
given offence to God. But there is nothing to be done save live
virtuously and pray.'

'Alas!' exclaimed the Frenchman, whereupon Tala, annoyed
maybe to find his own despondency matched, threatened him with
a pistol but did not fire it.

At the barrier, the Queen's guards challenged them: 'What are
you?'

'Friends of my Lord Bothwell's.'

'What was that crack?' (explosion) asked the sentry.

'We know not.'

'If you are friends of my Lord Bothwell's go your way.'

On reaching his lodging, Bothwell called for a drink, undressed
and went to bed. It would be about half past two in the morning.
Hepburn lay for a while on a bed in Bothwell's hall; after that he
and Tala went off to spend the night in Hepburn's house in the
Canongate.

About three o'clock the Earl's rest was disturbed by the arrival of
one George Hackett, who made a great noise at his gate demanding

admittance. When the gate was opened, Hackett was seen to be speechless with terror and breathlessness, and (thought Powrie) as black as the ace of spades.

'What's the matter, man?' asked Bothwell.

'The King's house is blown up,' panted Hackett, 'and I believe the King is killed.'

'Treason!' cried Bothwell, beginning to pull on his clothes.

9 Nine men at the deed

SMALL WONDER THAT THE murder of Lord Darnley has led to controversy and speculation through the centuries! What a reckless, clumsy, and amateurish business! Candles bought at the last minute from a shop a few yards from the scene of the crime! Another candle borrowed from a cook who was not a party to the conspiracy! Could anything be more imprudent—unless it was the presence of a naked flame in a small room (sixteen feet by twelve) where gunpowder was being tipped into a heap on the floor? A barrel brought to the house and discarded in the yard outside where it would inevitably be found and traced to its origin. The fourfold announcement that men claiming to be friends of Lord Bothwell's were abroad in the streets before and immediately after the explosion!

Short of an open avowal of the murder, it is hard to see what more Bothwell and his associates could have done to attract suspicion to themselves.

Some historians, in their perplexity, have been driven to seek alternative explanations of the events of that night. One student[1] convinced himself that the powder was not placed in Kirk o' Field to blow up Darnley but, on the contrary, was put there with Darnley's knowledge, to blow up the Queen. Instead of there being a plot to rid Mary of a husband she detested, there was a conspiracy by Catholic fanatics to rid Scotland of a queen who (so the theory runs) fell short of what was required from her by the extreme protagonists of the Counter-Reformation.

Having stowed away enough explosive in his house to blow it sky-high, Darnley was to wait some convenient occasion when the

1. Major-General R. H. Mahon in *The Tragedy of Kirk o' Field*, Cambridge University Press, Cambridge 1930.

Queen was there—and then slip out discreetly, leaving his wife to be murdered. The occasion was thought to have come on that Sunday night.

Darnley, according to this theory, expected Mary to return from the Palace after Bastien's wedding masque; indeed she meant to do so until, at that long private conference, Bothwell (who had, somehow, come to suspect Darnley's intentions) and John Stewart of Traquair persuaded her not to do so. After that, Bothwell and his band, with righteous indignation in their hearts, went up to Kirk o' Field to deal out justice to the intending assassin. Somehow, the slow match was lighted and Darnley, seeking to escape from his own mine, was strangled along with his servant and left, under a pear-tree, on the ground just outside the Town Wall.

It must be said, alas, that there is not a scrap of evidence for this fascinating story, no reason in the world to suppose that Darnley put a charge of gunpowder under his own bedroom with a slow match ready to the hand of anyone with a fancy for explosions.

It may be admitted that the agents of the Counter-Reformation did not always have the most realistic opinions in political matters. There was, about this time, a widespread delusion among the more hot-headed clergy, that, if only a handful of men could be disposed of, the whole business of stamping out heresy would be greatly expedited. A common thread of passionate unreason unites these ecclesiastics.

The confessor of the Duc de Montpensier, writing in the year of Darnley's murder, had no doubt of the best way of dealing with the Huguenot problem in France: 'The shortest cure would be to cut off the heads of Condé, the Admiral, Andelot, Gramont and La Rochefoucauld.' How closely this thinking was echoed in the letter which Laureo, Papal Nuncio to Scotland, wrote to the Cardinal of Alessandria on August 21, 1566: 'The difficulties might be obviated if justice were executed against six rebels, the Earls of Moray and Argyll, the Earl of Morton, the Laird of Lethington; Bellenden, Justice Clerk and James Macgill, Clerk Register.'

In this letter, evidence has been found to support the opinion that Darnley intended Kirk o' Field as a plot against his wife. The argument runs that Mary rejected the bloodthirsty advice of the Nuncio, who then turned to her husband as a more reliable instrument of papal policy. If others perished in the gunpowder plot besides the Queen, so much the better!

It must be pointed out, however, that of the six men named in the Nuncio's letter only one, Argyll, was in Kirk o' Field at any time during that evening.

Even the most wrong-headed and unscrupulous of Catholic conspirators in Europe can be exculpated of any design to replace Mary Stuart by her husband.

The Queen might indeed appear to have less zeal in the faith than was satisfactory to Rome or the Escorial. But she was the Queen of Scots, a creature of high qualities and many graces. She was, too, a devoted daughter of the Church. Darnley was a vicious, unpleasant and, probably, unhealthy coxcomb. The idea that any Jesuit in his senses would prefer the husband to the wife as a champion of the Catholic cause is preposterous.

There was, too, one powerful reason why the King of Spain, leader of the Catholic Reaction in Europe, should at that time be anxious to encourage no action against the Queen of Scots. He was preparing a military enterprise of great delicacy and moment: a veteran Spanish army was about to march northwards, along a route about seven hundred miles in length from Italy to Flanders, skirting the borders of France. While it was on the move, the expeditionary force would be vulnerable to a French flanking attack.

In France, Philip had fierce enemies, the Huguenots, doubtful friends, like Catherine de' Medici, and staunch allies, the Guises. Was it likely that he would weaken the prestige of these friends, or incur their enmity by plotting against Mary Stuart, herself a Guise and a cherished instrument of the family's policies? The arrival of the Spanish troops in Brussels and Antwerp was a strategic event of capital importance made possible by diplomatic negotiations at the time of Darnley's murder. To realise it, Philip would sacrifice or postpone any undertaking in a minor theatre like Scotland.

Yet the fanciful idea of a plot against the Queen, disastrously miscarrying to confound its devisors, serves one useful purpose: it encourages a closer inspection of the story of the murder as it was told by the men who confessed they had committed it.

In the foregoing pages, a single narrative has been spun out of strands of testimony given by different men, on different occasions spread over many months, before different judges who had only the most limited opportunities to check one deposition against another. Inevitably there are discrepancies.

Powrie says at first that the gunpowder was carried by two horses in one journey and, on re-examination, agrees that there was only one horse which made two journeys. It is hardly likely Powrie would have forgotten a detail of this kind. On the other hand, there is no obvious reason for him to falsify the story in this way. The most likely explanation is that Powrie, through stupidity or plain carelessness or an understandable anxiety to shorten the disagreeable business of interrogation, gave at first an abbreviated version of the night's work. Or, possibly, his first account was so confused that his interrogators misunderstood him.

There is other evidence to support the view that Powrie was not a man of marked intelligence. Sometime during the course of the evening, he had the imprudence to warn an acquaintance named William Geddes not to be found on the street that night. It was friendly counsel, but likely to be remembered to Powrie's disadvantage. It was.

Given the confused and crowded nature of these hours in the darkened streets of Edinburgh, the comings and goings, groupings and re-groupings of the characters, the various accounts agree well enough.

On two issues there are graver doubts:

Would two horse-loads of gunpowder—say, two hundredweights—in a heap on the floor of a small room make a powerful enough explosion to wreck a building and kill some, at least, of those inside it?

The opinion of modern experts is divided, one school (the Royal Engineers) holding that, unless the powder were contained in a barrel, the job could not be done; another (the Home Office) maintaining that two hundredweights is a big heap of gunpowder. Were the room small enough, the ceiling low enough and the building in bad repair, an explosion of surprising force might be produced.

But would the force be enough to blow Darnley and his servant Will Taylor through the roof of Kirk o' Field and over the town wall of Edinburgh, so that their bodies were found forty feet from where their beds had been? Most surprising of all, an explosion powerful enough to do this, left no outward sign of injury or blackening upon the two victims. (A third body was found in the ruins of the house, badly mangled.)

The testimony for this curious circumstance is impressive.

Various conjectures have been put forward: that Darnley and his servant were smothered in bed, or alternatively that, taking alarm at noises they heard in the house, they rushed outside in their nightclothes to be strangled there. After that the explosion occurred —or, perhaps, was made to occur by the criminals in order to destroy the evidence of what they had done. These notions can be disposed of quickly.

If Darnley and Taylor were smothered in bed, why were they not left there to be buried in the ruins made by the explosion? If there was going to be an explosion, why did anyone take the trouble to smother them? If the explosion was induced as a means of hiding, or confusing, evidence, why were the bodies of the victims laid out, naked and conspicuous, under the pear-tree? If they were strangled, why did they exhibit none of the signs of strangulation, which are spectacular and easily recognised?

On the whole, it is easier to believe that Darnley was killed by the explosion and was saved by his bed from the blackening effects of the blast. That there was a freakish element in the explosion may be acknowledged. Bothwell himself was obviously puzzled that there was no mark on the bodies. But that the explosion was the agency of the murder seems most closely in accordance with the evidence.

Six years and ten months after the event,[1] Black Ormiston made a confession in Edinburgh Castle to John Brand, minister of the Canongate Kirk. He was about to be executed. Ormiston then insisted that Darnley was not touched by any man's hands. The Laird was not, according to his own story, present at Kirk o' Field when the explosion occurred but he would certainly know what his associates thought had happened.

Just a year after the murder, Hepburn of Bowton made his confession shortly before he was hanged at the Mercat Cross of Edinburgh. There were nine and no more at the deed, he said, and if the King was handled by anyone it was not by them. It can be assumed, then, that the men of Bothwell's party that night sincerely

1. December 13, 1573.

believed they had blown Darnley up and killed him. Kirk o' Field was a gunpowder plot.

There is, however, another question: Were the nine, whose names are known, the only evilly disposed men near Darnley's lodging that night?

Mrs. Crockett and Mrs. Martin, independent witnesses, who certainly saw the group come down from Kirk o' Field and even reported correctly that it split into two at the Cowgate, agreed that the men who hurried past them numbered eleven. The night was dark, the glimpse was brief, and, after so loud an explosion, the women may have been nervous. But William Powrie speaks of two men muffled in cloaks seen but not identified by him near Black-friars' Gate. Who were they? Sir James Balfour come with his brother Robert to see how the work he had helped to plan was going forward? Or Mr. Archibald Douglas, later the parson of Glasgow, who was thought to have lost a slipper at Kirk o' Field that night, and his servant John Binning, who was hanged in Edinburgh fourteen years later for his part in the murder, whatever that part may have been? Lord Huntly, Lord Argyll, who had an inkling of what was afoot? The questions cannot be answered.

There is, in any case, no real discrepancy between Hepburn's insistence that nine men were at work under Bothwell's orders and that other men were lurking in the neighbourhood. After all, Bothwell was certainly right in claiming that he was not the sole principal in the project which he and Sir James Balfour planned and which he and his eight companions carried out. And it is possible that some of the other parties sent their representatives to the scene as they had probably promised Bothwell they would do.

Darnley had six servants within call. Had there been a scuffle, it would be important to overwhelm his supporters. If there turned out to be no need to intervene, then the watchers could melt away in the labyrinth of Edinburgh's wynds and closes. This would certainly be in conformity with the character of a man like Sir James Balfour, wicked enough for any mischief, craftier and more cautious by far than Bothwell.

One graver question remains: what pre-knowledge did Mary have of the attempt against her husband's life?

If Casket Letter II is ignored, then evidence against the Queen *up to the time of the murder* is circumstantial but by no means conclusive.

She disliked and distrusted Darnley. She had conceived a passion for Bothwell who had become, with her approval, the most powerful of her ministers. Between the two of them there was a constant flow of private messages, through Tala, through French Paris and, maybe, through others. Another statement by Paris, during his second examination, should also be noted: that while Darnley was at Kirk o' Field, Bothwell visited the Queen night after night. He was led to her room by Lady Reres, while John Hepburn kept watch under the galleries of the Palace.

Paris may have invented this story to please his interrogators, whose main interest would be to damage Mary's reputation. But it falls in with the notion given in Casket Letter II that Lady Reres was an object of Darnley's hatred. It supplies a reason why this might be so. If Mary was, as the Letter suggests and Paris testified, actually carrying on an adulterous amour with Bothwell, then it becomes more likely that she knew Darnley was to be killed.

In the relations between the Queen and her lover one other circumstance may be noted: Mary was jealous. In the Letter she spoke with hatred of Bothwell's young wife. Paris, in his second examination, declares Bothwell forbade him on his life to tell the Queen his wife was staying with him in the Palace. As a jealous mistress, Mary was liable to make scenes. And as a jealous mistress, she would be anxious to show her devotion to her lover.

Whether this was her motive or not, it was certainly Mary who went to Glasgow and persuaded her husband to return to Edinburgh. She did so at a time when she and Darnley were on the worst of terms and when it would still be too early for the convalescent, if he made the journey, to stay at the Palace when he arrived. If she had not done so, using all her charm and intelligence for the purpose, Darnley would not have lodged at Kirk o' Field on February 9, 1567, and the murder would not have taken place.

In Edinburgh no doubt existed in anyone's mind about the identity of those who were most closely concerned with Darnley's murder. The main question was, what part had the Queen in the crime? This question Mary lost no time in answering in a way which the burgesses of Edinburgh found completely convincing.

After all, the town was small and compact. It had a population of probably about 10,000 if the inhabitants of the court suburb of the Canongate are left out of the reckoning. No doubt, in its taverns and lodging houses there was a flock of birds of passage up for a few days to buy weapons or sell beasts. It was a market town as well as being the seat of government. It is a fact highly relevant to the evolution of events that Darnley was assassinated in a crowded little town where ears were keen and tongues were busy.

Bothwell and his confederates had dropped clues all over Edinburgh like drunk sailors scattering their money. The servants in the Palace may have said no word about strange comings and goings they had noticed. The sentries at the Palace gates may have kept a soldierly silence about the movements of 'my Lord Bothwell's friends' that night.

But what of the man above Sandy Bruce's closehead who supplied Tala's servant with an empty powder barrel—and, no doubt, recognised it outside Kirk o' Field? What of Geordie Bruce's wife in the Cowgate who sold Powrie half a dozen candles a few hours before the explosion? Was it likely that John Galloway, keeper of Nethergow Port, would keep his mouth shut about his late visitors? Katy's Tam Henderson may have known nothing of his tenant Black Ormiston's doings that Sunday night but, at the foot of the turnpike stair, Ade Murray and some others saw Bothwell, a nobleman they would certainly know by sight, in company with Tala, a young laird who was probably a familiar enough figure near Ormiston's lodging. The meeting would be impressed on their mind when Bothwell roughly sent them about their business. Before the night ended, Murray and his companions may well have recalled the incident, even if they had the discretion to do so in whispers.

There was also William Geddes who remembered that his friend Powrie, whom he would know as one of Lord Bothwell's servants, had given him the friendly advice not to be found on the street that night. And, of course, there were those wakeful matrons, Mrs. Martin and Mrs. Crockett, who could claim to have seen and counted the assassins a few seconds after the explosion.

When the people of Edinburgh emerged, timorously or curiously into the streets, when the town watch marched on Kirk o' Field and found the appalling evidence of regicide, there would be no lack of hints and clues to link one with another. Before dawn came, it is reasonable to suppose that Edinburgh had formed ideas of its own about the sequence of events.

Why was Bothwell so careless? The answer is surely not hard to find. Scotland was passing through a moral and spiritual revolution in which political ends might be sought by criminal means and crimes might not be punished if the policies they served were triumphant.

Eleven months before the murder of Darnley, Edinburgh was the scene of an even more spectacular crime. The royal Palace was stormed and captured by a force at the head of which was a group of the first nobles in the land. The Queen's most trusted servant was brutally murdered within her sight or, at least, within her hearing. She herself was threatened by the pistol of one of the ruffians. She would have been compelled, in a day or two, to accept the findings of a packed Parliament convened in order to vindicate the conspirators. By an extraordinary turn in events, the plot collapsed and the Queen was restored. But not one man of note suffered for his part in the affair.

A minor figure was executed. Ker of Fawdonside, who had threatened to kill the Queen, was kept under guard in a Border keep. The Earl of Morton was still forbidden the court. That was all. Where the law was lame, moral condemnation was even more feeble: John Knox, prophet and conscience of the emergent Scotland, found the killing of Riccio 'worthy of all praise'.

Why then, need Bothwell, having seen how the perpetrators of the earlier murder had escaped, take any pains to hide his tracks in the later? He was the most powerful nobleman in the land, master of the Queen's council, in all likelihood sharer of her bed. Soon he would be greater still. Juries could be packed. It was the custom of the age. Parliament could be packed. It had happened before. Edinburgh could be overawed by well-armed professional soldiers recruited for the purpose. Reckless, unscrupulous, overweening, what had Lord Bothwell to fear?

The Queen's position seemed even more unassailable. Bothwell's hand in the murder might be guessed. Her part could be suspected only by persons endowed with exceptional malice or special information. The Letters were still safe in their casket. The secrets they contained were not yet revealed as truths, acted out in deeds before they were read in words, dishonouring, destroying. And without the Letters, what could be proved against the woman? Who would dare to accuse the Queen?

It seems that, during the days which immediately followed her husband's murder, Mary lived in a world where only her passion was real. She did not defy the dangers round her, rather, she was unaware of them. The dangers were—what? The surprising coolness of foreign courts. The jealousy of officials. The withdrawal from Court of important members of the nobility. Between these and Mary stood Bothwell and his musketeers. As for the grim mouths and mutinous eyes of the people, they mattered not at all.

There could have been no greater miscalculation.

10 *A cry in the night*

ON THE DAY OF Darnley's murder, Mary wrote an account of the outrage to her ambassador in Paris, Archbishop Beaton.

'It was designed as well for ourself as for the King,' she wrote, 'for we lay for the most part of all last week in that same lodging (and was there accompanied with the most part of the lords that are in this Town) and that same night, at midnight, and of very chance tarried not all night [there], by reason of some masque at the Abbey [i.e. Holyrood], but we believe it was not chance but God that put it in our head.'

On the same day, fifteen members of the Scottish Council met in urgent session in Holyroodhouse. Their task was to devise a report for Catherine de' Medici, Queen-Mother of France, formerly Mary's mother-in-law.

'The authors of this crime,' they said, 'very nearly destroyed the Queen in the same way—with most of the Lords at present in her suite—who had been with the King in his chamber until nearly midnight. Her majesty might easily have remained there all night, but God has been so gracious to us that these assassins have been despoiled of a part of their prey and has reserved her majesty to take the vengeance which such a barbarous and inhuman act deserves.'

Signed by the fifteen councillors present, the most notable of whom were Bothwell, Huntly, Argyll and Lethington, the letter was given to a French diplomat, the Seigneur de Clernault, who set off to Paris with all suitable speed. Passing through London, he gave his own account: 'About 2 a.m. a tremendous noise was heard, as of a volley of twenty-five or thirty cannon, arousing the whole town . . . the King's lodging totally destroyed, and himself sixty or eighty steps from the house in a garden, dead. . . . One may imagine the distress and agony of this poor princess. . . .'

Another circumstance must, however, have made an even stronger impression on those who read the narratives. Since Mary had left Kirk o' Field with all due ceremony and display three hours before the explosion occurred, it was hard to see how the assassins could have intended to kill her as well as Darnley. Even among historians favourable to the Queen, this apparent absurdity in her narrative has been held against her.

Had she not noticed that Paris was grimy with the powder he had been handling that night? The incident is mentioned in the memoir which Claude Nau, her personal secretary, prepared probably under her supervision. If Paris was reasonably suspected, why was he not put instantly to the question? And could there be any doubt in Mary's mind that, if Paris was involved, Bothwell was implicated as well? But Bothwell, whatever else he may have done, certainly did not try to kill Mary at Kirk o' Field when he knew very well she was at Holyrood. In that case, the accounts sent to the Archbishop and to Catherine de' Medici seem at least to lack candour.

The news of the assassination spread all over Europe, and, wherever it went, wild rumours followed. The Savoy ambassador, Sieur di Moretta, whose farewell supper party had been so closely followed by the tragedy, made known the opinion in Paris when he arrived there that Darnley had been smothered in the garden while trying to escape from the imminent danger of explosion. The Jesuit Father Edmund who travelled with the ambassador passed on to the Papal Nuncio the edifying tidings that Darnley had heard mass that Sunday morning as was his custom.

Giovanni Corrier, the Venetian ambassador in Paris, picked up Moretta's story and conveyed it to the Signory of the republic with some embellishments. According to this version Darnley, taking fright, lowered himself from a window into the garden where he was surrounded by assailants and 'strangled with the sleeves of his own shirt'. The assassins then blew up his sleeping quarters, hoping it would be believed that Darnley had been killed in falling from the window in a frantic attempt to escape. Correr's report went on:

'It was widely rumoured that the principal persons in the kingdom were implicated . . . and above all a bastard brother of the Queen' (the Earl of Moray) 'is suspected because, at the time when she was

The Earl of Moray, half-brother of Mary Stuart

A portrait by Munro

at variance with her husband, the bastard told her that the King had boasted to him of having had intimacy with her before she was his wife. The Queen, exasperated, asked the King if it was true. The King gave the lie to the said bastard, who repeated the accusation to the King's face . . . From this private quarrel the report arose that the bastard had desired to revenge himself.'

It may be that Correr and Moretta between them have garbled a story which has some element of truth. After all, Mary had other bastard brothers besides Moray. There is some evidence that there had been a violent quarrel between Darnley and her half-brother Lord Robert Stewart a day or two before the murder. The Queen's enemies alleged, later on, that Mary had fomented the quarrel, seeing in it a convenient way of disposing of her husband.

French Paris, in his second and more forthcoming deposition, said that the Queen sent him to Bothwell on Saturday, February 8, with the message: 'It seems to me it would be better if Lord Robert Stewart and William Blackadder went to the King's room to do what Bothwell knows.'

William Blackadder was a sea-captain and probably an associate of Bothwell's. He was certainly in Edinburgh on the night of the murder, in which he had no part whatever, as he insisted strenuously later, on his way to the scaffold.

Bothwell, according to the story of Paris, listened to Mary's suggestion and said he would talk to Lord Robert and then to the Queen. In any case, nothing came of this proposal, if it were ever made.

The Spanish ambassador in London, Guzman de Silva, heard about the murder from Sir Robert Melville, Mary's envoy, who had been overtaken by the news on his way south and returned to Edinburgh for fresh instructions.

'I asked him some questions,' writes the Spaniard, 'to try to get at the bottom of the suspicion as to who had been the author of the crime but could get nothing definite. Even if the Queen clears herself from it, the matter is still obscure. . . . The case is a very strange one, and has greatly grieved the Catholics.'

One person had no doubt that Mary had a hand in the affair: Darnley's mother, the Countess of Lennox, locked in the Tower of London by Elizabeth because her son had married the Queen of Scots, and now, in her passionate sorrow, released. To Melville,

Lady Lennox poured out a torrent of accusation against Mary. 'Grief like this distracts the most prudent people,' remarked de Silva, 'much more one so sorely beset.'

Before the end of February, it was apparent that Mary's position in Europe had been immeasurably damaged. Of all the foreign observers of the crisis in Scotland, Elizabeth was the most understanding, the best informed and the most nervous. Some precautions she took at once. All the keys of doors leading to her room were taken away. The loyalty of the guard on her palace was investigated. What had been done in Edinburgh might be attempted at Westminster.

There was, too, a danger of another kind. If Mary's reputation were besmirched, then the prestige of queens everywhere would be lowered. If Mary were to lose the respect of her subjects, so that she was deposed—and even put on trial—precedents most alarming for Elizabeth would be created.

She wrote to the widow, grieving more for her, she explained, than for the dead man: 'I should not do the office of a faithful cousin and friend, if I did not urge you to preserve your honour . . . I write thus vehemently not that I doubt, but for affection.'

From Archbishop Beaton in Paris an outburst of horror and supplication reached Mary: 'Alas, Madame, this day over all Europe there is no purpose in head so frequent as that of your majesty and of the present estate of your realm!' Echoing the known opinions of Catherine de' Medici, he implored his young sovereign: 'Do such justice as to the whole world may declare your innocence.'

Wise and indeed essential advice which, during the critical weeks and months that followed Mary did not, and perhaps could not, follow.

In Edinburgh whispers grew into rumours. One after another the conspirators were troubled in courage or conscience. French Paris was the first to give way. His miserable, hangdog mien irritated Bothwell, who, the day after the murder, upbraided him angrily, 'Why do you look like that? Look at these gentlemen,' meaning Ormiston and the others, 'who have lands, rents and revenues, wives and children, and were willing to give up everything in my service. If you think you have offended God, the sin is not yours but mine.'

Paris took his troubles to the Queen: people were looking at him askance. Mary told him not to worry.

When Black Ormiston's conscience began to prick him, powerfully assisted by the rumours that were rising, he said to Bothwell, 'What the devil is this now? Everybody suspects you!' Bothwell showed him a contract which seemed to bear the signatures of Huntly, Argyll, Lethington and Sir James Balfour. 'Whoever took the deed in hand, they will defend it as if they had done it themselves,' he said.

The general horror and condemnation which the crime aroused seems to have taken the murderers by surprise. Why, after all, should one man's death in an age of violence be the occasion of so much revulsion? Hay of Tala, shunned by respectable people, was a prey to unaccustomed soul-searching. One day when they were staying at Lord Seton's house a few miles east of Edinburgh, Bothwell asked him, 'What did you think when you saw him blown up?' Tala shuddered. 'Alas, my lord, why do you say that? Whenever I hear such a thing, the words wound me to the death, as they should you.'

It is quite likely that the young Laird, on whose confession before execution this story depends, did say something of the sort to his leader, although the remark may not have had the sanctimonious ring which he gave it, in reminiscence. Fear rather than piety probably weighed on his spirits at Seton that day.

Fear, or at least a reasonable prudence, impelled John Hepburn of Bowton during the days after the crime. The false keys of Kirk o' Field made on Bothwell's orders were left in his keeping. He dropped them into a quarry-hole between 'the Abbey' and Leith.

Having stronger nerves than his collaborators, Bothwell put a bolder face on events. He walked the streets of Edinburgh, looking every man hard in the eye, his hand on his sword, bodyguards about him, fierce Borderers, armed to the teeth. His need for them was real.

Mary's conduct at this time failed to satisfy the watchful eyes in Scotland and straining ears abroad. Outwardly she comported herself as a widowed queen should, receiving her guests in a room draped in black with curtains drawn, spending £60 on serge of Florence for a mourning gown, cloak, mules and shoes, and £40 on drugs and spices for perfuming 'the king's grace majesty's umquhile[1] body'. Her apothecary, a Frenchman, Martin Picavet, signed the receipt for this money.

It is possible that, during those post-mortem offices, the discovery was made that one of Darnley's ribs had been broken by the explosion and that he had suffered grave internal injuries. This information reached the Papal Legate in Paris in a letter which Mary wrote on February 16 and dispatched by the hand of her trusted valet Sebastien Pages.

On Thursday, February 13, the Islay Herald, Peter Thomson, fixed to the Mercat Cross of Edinburgh a proclamation offering £2000 Scots to anyone who would 'declare' the King's murderer. There was no lack of persons who thought they could throw light on the business, although not all of them were anxious to come forward. However, the lords of the Queen's council listened to the sworn and voluble testimonies of Mrs. Martin and Mrs. Crockett, who seem to have enjoyed the attention they had brought on themselves.

Thomas Nelson, one of Darnley's valets, who had survived the explosion, was questioned about the events of the night, especially about what had happened to the keys of the house. He said that the Queen's usher, Archibald Beaton, had the keys of her room and Bonkil, the cook, the key of the cellar. At this point the Laird of Tullibardine interrupted: 'Hold there! He is aground!' No more questions were asked.

The murder remained unexplained, although interest in it was kept alive. The Queen went to stay at Lord Seton's house from which reports reached Edinburgh of her carefree demeanour, and worst of all that Bothwell was in her company.

The Scottish capital was prepared to think the worst of its widowed sovereign, so long as she consorted with a man who was believed to have had some part in her husband's death. Mary, who must have known of the belief, treated it as a matter with which she, a queen, need feel no concern. If she was waiting on time to calm her subjects' suspicions, then she was disappointed.

Sunday after Sunday the preachers implored the Almighty to reveal and revenge the murder of the King. Night after night, a strange fanatical cry echoed through the streets of the town calling for 'vengeance on those who caused me to shed innocent blood. Lord, open the heavens and pour down vengeance on me and those

1. Sc. former.

that have destroyed the innocent!' Who was responsible for this eerie nocturnal visitation is not recorded. But its effects on the nerves of the citizens, already disturbed by what had happened, can be imagined.

A day came when the well-informed Sir William Drury, Queen Elizabeth's Marshal of Berwick, reported to his chief, Cecil, in London: 'The man that walked up and down the streets in the night with the cry of vengeance for the murder is now apprehended and shut up in a prison which they call, for the loathsomeness of the place, "the foul thief's pit".'

He might be silenced, that anonymous miscreant or madman, but he had done his share in keeping alive the alarm of Edinburgh.

Another report, even more sinister, reached Drury at his listening post in Berwick. It said that a servant of Sir James Balfour's had been secretly killed and buried on the 'lively presumption' that he had made, through 'remorse or other folly', some injudicious disclosures about the murder.

To the accompaniment of such events or rumours, the menacing wails from the pulpits of the town were all the more impressive. Reveal and revenge!

The situation was not without its irony—if anyone had been in the mood for so detached an exercise! Darnley had been a Catholic, although not particularly faithful or devout. He had probably toyed with conspiracy in the Catholic interest. Now, dead, he became an instrument of anti-Catholic propaganda, skilfully, powerfully and unscrupulously reiterated.

A few days after Islay Herald had put up the proclamation at the Cross, some unknown person pinned a reply to the door of the Tolbooth, nearby. He had enquired about the murderers. Now he could identify them: the Earl Bothwell, Mr. James Balfour, Mr. David Chalmers, and Black Mr. John Spens who was the chief planner. Further, the placard said that the Queen had assented to the murder, through Bothwell's influence and the witchcraft of the Lady Buccleuch who had at one time been Bothwell's mistress. If anyone doubted these revelations, he had only to ask Gilbert Balfour (a brother of Sir James Balfour).

The poster campaign against Bothwell continued and had its effect. Elizabeth's ambassador Killigrew sent word to London that he found great suspicion, no proof and 'a general misliking among the commons'. James Murray of Purdovis, a brother of Tullibardine and an old enemy of Bothwell, was denounced by the Privy Council for having fixed 'certain printed papers' to the door of the Edinburgh Tolbooth 'tending to her majesty's slander'. One poster had 'M.R.' in large Roman letters with a sword in hand near it, and 'L.B.' (Lord Bothwell) and a mallet. Another spoke of a smith who had made the duplicate keys for Kirk o' Field and was ready to identify the assassins.

Bothwell, going about with his guard of fifty retainers, swore that, if he knew who put up the posters, he would wash his hands in their blood. Sir James Balfour took the precaution of surrounding himself with armed servants.

More serious than the posters was a letter to the Queen from Lord Lennox, father of the murdered man, asking for the arrest and trial of Bothwell, Balfour, and half a dozen other suspects. This challenge could hardly be ignored. Accordingly, on Good Friday, the Privy Council named April 12 as the day on which the Court of Judiciary would try Bothwell and anyone suspected as his accomplice. In a letter signed that day by the Queen, Lennox was directed to attend.

It had been, for Mary, a Holy Week full of incident. On Palm Sunday, mass was sung for Darnley's soul in the chapel royal at Holyrood at which the Queen seems to have broken down more than once. Later, recovering her spirits, she gave some valuable church vestments to Bothwell.

At six o'clock on the morning of Bothwell's trial the Provost Marshal of Berwick, who had ridden through the night, arrived at Holyrood with a letter to Mary from her royal cousin in London. He was told that the Queen could not be disturbed. When he came back to the Palace between nine and ten, he found the forecourt filled with mounted nobles and gentlemen. He handed over the letter to Lethington who took it into the Queen.

Emerging half an hour later with Bothwell, he was about to brush past the Provost Marshal without speaking when the Englishman pushed forward: Had the Queen's majesty read the letter? What answer was he to take back? Lethington told him the Queen was still asleep so the letter had not been delivered. It must now wait until after the trial. Whereupon the cavalcade, numbering as some thought as many as 4000 horsemen, set off with a lusty cheer for the Tolbooth. With them, in the midst of 200 musketeers, rode the accused Lord Bothwell.

In the letter which Mary had, perhaps, failed to read that morning, her cousin of England renewed with passionate entreaty counsel which she had already given: 'For the love of God, Madam, use such sincerity and prudence in this case which touches you so closely, that all the world shall have reason to pronounce you innocent of a crime of such enormity, a thing which, if you do it not, you would deserve to fall from the ranks of Princesses, and, not without cause, become opprobrious to the people; and, rather than that should happen to you, I would wish you an honourable burial than a soiled life.'

Some critics have found this letter an offensive and outrageous interference in Scottish affairs, cunningly designed to weaken Mary's government and strengthen its adversaries. It seems at least arguable that Elizabeth's purpose was less malignant.

She may have believed in Mary's innocence at this time, as Moray—who made Mary guardian of his only child—may also have done. It is more likely, however, that purely political interests prevailed and that the daughter of Henry VIII was concerned that her sister queen should have enough gumption to *prove* herself innocent.

In the Tolbooth of Edinburgh, Archibald, Earl of Argyll, Lord Justice-General of Scotland, presided over the court that heard the indictment against Bothwell. The farce was played out with all becoming solemnity, although it was shorn of some of its drama by reason of the absence of the chief witness for the prosecution, the Earl of Lennox.

As chancellor, or foreman, of the jury, George Sinclair, Earl of Caithness, was chosen. This nobleman, a Catholic but a friend of Bothwell's, was probably not able to give his full attention to the grave matter before the court. Other questions were, about that time, occupying his mind. In three months his cousin Isobel Sinclair would, at his instigation, poison the Earl and Countess of Sutherland.

The new young Earl, aged fifteen, was then put under the tutelage of Caithness, who married the boy to his daughter, a woman aged thirty-two of dubious reputation. Behind these manœuvres lay not some motiveless spite but solid considerations of the ownership of land.

Caithness was a man with lofty notions of family loyalty. When his son took sides with his enemies the Murrays, he kept the young man in a dungeon, fed him on salt beef and denied him water until he died.

A man of such principles would be unlikely to strain the evidence against his friend Bothwell. But, as it turned out, there was no evidence.

Robert Cunningham, a servant of the absent Earl of Lennox, explained that his master did not appear because he was afraid for his life, and protested that any judgment arrived at by the jury would be in error.

Undeterred, the jury of fifteen peers and lairds withdrew and after prolonged deliberation acquitted Bothwell of 'art and part of the said slaughter of the King'. Following this not unexpected verdict Bothwell was greeted by the acclamation of his friends inside and outside the court. Cunningham, it may be assumed, did not unduly prolong his stay in so unpropitious a neighbourhood.

Next day, Bothwell posted up a challenge in Edinburgh, offering to fight any person who dared to maintain that he was guilty of the murder. He had three anonymous accepters. The first supplied, in writing, a choice list of desperadoes—seven who planned and twelve who performed the deed—and appended a few lines of doggerel:

> 'It is not enough the poor king is dead
> But the mischand[1] murderers occupy his stead
> And double adultery has all the land shamed.'

The third poster adopted a loftier, more theological, theme: 'There is none that profess Christ and His Evangel that can with upright conscience part Bothwell and his wife, albeit she prove him an abominable adulterer and worse, as he has murdered the husband of her he intends to marry, whose promise he had long before the murder.'

It is obvious then that, whatever hopes Bothwell and Mary might have pinned to a formal clearance at law, they were disappointed.

1. Wicked.

Their situation was worse than it had been. What had been whispered and hinted about Mary was now in black and white on a placard fixed to the Town Cross of Edinburgh, seen by many of the citizens and reported to all of them.

The events that followed with vertiginous speed accomplished more than a thousand posters could have done to convince the public of the Queen's complicity. A week after the trial, Bothwell gave supper to a number of prelates and nobles in Ainslie's Tavern in the Canongate, a hostelry which has apparently left no other record in history. From this company he obtained a written promise that they would do all they could to advance his marriage to their sovereign whose need for support and comfort in her widowed state was manifest to all.

The signatories included the primate of Scotland, a sordid scoundrel; the Earl of Huntly whose sister was at that moment the wife of Bothwell; the Earl of Argyll who was married to Mary's half-sister; the Earl of Cassillis, head of the Kennedys, and, young as he was, second to none in perfidy and bloodthirstiness even in that grim company; the Earl of Morton, celebrated for avarice and lust, a party to the murder of Riccio, an accessory to the murder of Darnley and, in due course, to add fresh distinctions to these; the Earl of Caithness, a future murderer and president of the jury that had found Bothwell an innocent man.

Protestant and Catholic, they sat round the table at Ainslie's while the wine flowed and the talk grew more jovial. And there, clergy and layman, they pledged their approval to the Queen's marriage to the man whom most of them believed to be her lover and chief assassin of her husband.

Should any of them have hesitated for a moment before signing, he had only to look out of the window where he would see the businesslike outline of one of Lord Bothwell's musketeers. A powerful argument, which could later become evidence for blackmail and duress. In spite of it, one of the peers, Eglinton, a Catholic, is said to have slipped away without signing.

Some days earlier, Mary and Bothwell had signed the marriage contract.

THE CLIMAX OF THE affair came five days after this carousing. Mary, who had been to visit her baby son at Stirling, spent the night at Linlithgow. Next day, April 24, she set off for Edinburgh accompanied by a retinue of thirty mounted gentlemen. A few miles west of the town, at a point where the road crosses the river Almond, the Queen was intercepted by Bothwell with a force of cavalry numbering some hundreds which he had assembled on the pretext of undertaking a punitive raid on that nest of robbers, Liddesdale.

Bothwell took Mary's horse by the bridle. He told her that a rebellion was imminent and, with all suitable mixture of deference and firmness, invited her to ride with him to Dunbar Castle, thirty miles to the east. The Queen obeyed. One of her party, James Borthwick, was less compliant. He rode to Edinburgh with news of the abduction. The tocsin was rung. The burgesses ran to arm. Two pieces of artillery were wheeled out of the castle and fired at Bothwell's horsemen. In vain! Keeping clear of the Town Wall by half a mile or so, the Queen in the midst of her captors spurred on to Dunbar which she reached at midnight.

Scotland was stunned and mystified by the news that its Queen had been carried off against her will and ravished. Very soon the matter became even harder to understand, for it appeared that Mary, Catholic and devout, contemplated marriage with Bothwell, who was a Protestant, unbending if scarcely pious, and was a married man into the bargain.

So far as the Scottish public was concerned, the incident was greeted with astonishment rather than horror. Only from one town, Aberdeen, notorious for its independence of outlook, did there come any offer of help to their ill-used sovereign. Could they, the burgesses enquired, do anything 'towards the reparation of the matter?' It seemed that they could not. For the most part, Scotland was content to wait, with patience, on the unfolding of events.

To what extent can this story of rape be taken at its face value? Some degree of scepticism seems to be called for.

First of all, there is the character of the woman to be considered. Mary was the victim of the most sensational political event of its kind since the rape of Lucrece. It is possible to imagine a scene in which Bothwell, 'with Tarquin's ravishing strides, towards his design moves like a ghost', although the ravishing strides covered about forty miles of Scottish roads and passed along the main streets of several villages.

But had Mary no opportunity of appealing to her subjects for rescue during this long prelude to the act of violation? Was she the kind of woman who would tamely acquiesce in her own dishonour? This is a question on which evidence is not lacking.

Four years before, she had unleashed the law, pitilessly, against a young French adorer who, in his inordinate passion had concealed himself in her bedroom. She had taken the field actively and enjoyably against the Earl of Huntly, when political advantage and rich booty offered. A year before her abduction, she had frustrated a savage *coup d'état* at Holyrood by ingeniously organising her own escape and boldly carrying it out.

She was still the same woman, as she had been then, passionate, nervous and proud, victim of a temperament that belonged to the heights or the depths, knowing the tears of hysteria and the excitement of sustained physical exertion, familiar with the smell of danger.

Nor is it necessary to rely solely on deductions from Mary's character. There is other evidence. French Paris, in his second deposition, said that Bothwell's dependent Black Ormiston arrived at Linlithgow Palace on the day before the Queen was abducted and had a long secret conversation with her. But, it may be said, Paris could have invented this incident so that, by incriminating the Queen, he might please his captors? This possibility must be reckoned with.

Far more impressive than the Frenchman's story are three letters from Kirkcaldy of Grange, the most famous Scottish soldier of the day, to his English correspondent, the Earl of Bedford. The first was written four days before the abduction. The Queen, says Kirkcaldy, had declared that she would lose France, England and Scotland for Bothwell. She would go with him to the end of the world in a white petticoat before she would leave him.

To whom were the words spoken, if they *were* spoken? The record does not say. Somehow, in their recklessness and their extravagance, they seem to ring true as an utterance of Mary's. Certainly, Kirkcaldy of Grange was incapable of inventing them. If, as may be, he had access to some source of gossip near the Queen, it was a reliable one.

On April 24 he wrote to tell Bedford that Bothwell's wife was going to part from her husband and that Bothwell meant to carry off the Queen that day—which Bothwell did. Two days later, the abduction being accomplished, Grange wrote once more. Mary was minded, he said, to cause Bothwell to ravish her, so that she might the sooner bring his marriage to an end, 'which she had promised before she caused murder her husband'.

The day that this letter was written, Lady Bothwell's petition for divorce opened before the Protestant Commissary Court of Edinburgh. Bessie Crawford, the co-respondent, was the daughter of a blacksmith at Haddington. As a sewing maid of Bothwell's wife, her gleaming black hair and lively black eyes had caught the Earl's attention. It appears that this liaison reached its natural climax in the steeple of Haddington Abbey not long before the Queen was brought to bed of Darnley's son. After hearing evidence for four days, the court found that Lady Bothwell had established her husband's adultery.

In the meantime, the Archbishop of St. Andrews, who had a year before given a dispensation allowing Bothwell to marry his wife in spite of their blood relationship, now commissioned a Catholic consistory court to determine whether Bothwell was, in fact, truly married in the eyes of the Church. After a two days' hearing the court—John Manderston, Canon of Dunbar, sitting alone—found that the marriage had been null from the beginning in the absence of a dispensation.

But, as many men have recalled, there *had* been a dispensation—this inconvenient fact was brushed aside! Nor was it likely to trouble the records of the consistory court, which heard no other nullity case but this and, indeed, seems never to have met again.

Eight days after the annulment, Mary Stuart and James Hepburn were married in the great hall of Holyrood by Adam Bothwell, Bishop of Orkney, a Protestant but no relation of the bridegroom. There had been some trouble about the banns. The Rev. John Craig, minister of St. Giles' Kirk and, in the absence of John Knox, the senior ecclesiastic of the Calvinist Church in Edinburgh, had put forward a series of objections.

He had insisted on obtaining Mary's signature to a solemn declaration that she had not been abducted. He declined to act save at the command of the Kirk. Finally, he demanded an audience with the betrothed so that he could tell them what was in his mind. What was in John Craig's mind must have made unpleasant hearing for the Queen's hot-tempered lover.

'I laid to his charge,' said Craig, 'the law of adultery, the law of ravishing, the suspicion of collusion between him and his wife, the sudden divorce and proclaiming' (i.e. of the banns) 'within the space of four days, and last the suspicion of the King's death which his marriage would confirm.'

Bothwell kept a rein on his resentment, but Craig, far from satisfied in mind or conscience by the polite words with which his departure from the Palace had been speeded, touched on the matter in his sermon in St. Giles' next Sunday. In the hearing of the congregation he took heaven and earth to witness that he abhorred and detested a marriage that was odious and slanderous to the world.

The upright preacher was hauled before the Council and rebuked. He was not silenced: 'I answered the bounds of my Commission, which was the Word of God, good laws and natural reason, was able to prove whatever I spoke, yea that their own conscience . . .' But before John Craig could reach his proof, Bothwell told him to be silent and put him to the door.

Bothwell could not be unaware of the ominous overtones of Craig's civic and moral courage. On the day after the sermon, the Queen appeared in the Tolbooth of Edinburgh, a building that stood only a few yards from the church in which Craig had preached. She told the Lord Chancellor, the judges and other important officials that, while she had been angry with Bothwell for abducting her, his subsequent good behaviour had induced her to forgive him and his accomplices.

What useful purpose this act of pardon and oblivion was meant to serve may not be clear. One thing is certain, however: it would not satisfy the reason or conscience of those who thought like John Craig. Their number grew every day.

Preparations for the marriage went forward at a brisk pace. The Queen created Bothwell Duke of Orkney and Lord of Shetland, placing with her own hands the ducal coronet on his head. At the same time, four of his followers were knighted: James Cockburn of Langton, his cousin, Patrick Hay of Whitelaw, Patrick Hepburn of Boynston, and—surely most deserving the accolade of all, in the circumstances—Black Ormiston.

The wedding contract was drawn up in phrases that reflected credit on both parties: the Queen 'destitute of a husband' and 'humbly required to yield unto some marriage'; the new Duke, magnanimous, brave and constant in truth.

On the wedding day (Thursday, May 15) everything went smoothly and little attention was paid to the Latin tag fastened by some person unknown to the palace gates: 'The people say that wantons marry in the month of May.' The Queen was married in deep mourning, as she had been to Darnley. There was a fair sprinkling of nobility at the service—enough to call attention to the greater number who were absent. The French ambassador, Philibert du Croc, was not there. To all who could use eyes and ears it was obvious that a major clash in Scotland was not far off.

Various stories were put forward to explain this fatal marriage. By some, Bothwell was held to be a sorcerer who, by black arts that he had picked up from his old mistress, Lady Buccleuch, had gained an ascendancy over the Queen. Others thought that, having been violated by Bothwell at Dunbar, she had decided to make the best of things for the sake of the child she might be carrying.

The official account was conveyed to Catherine de' Medici in Paris by Mary's envoy the Bishop of Dunblane. Bothwell's behaviour, although rough, had proceeded from a mere excess of love. 'He would not agree to have the consummation of the marriage delayed but, as by a bravado he had won the first point, so ceased he never till by persuasion and importune suit, accompanied not the less by force, he has finally driven us to end the work begun.' In the Louvre this romantic story was received with Gallic derision.

The Venetian ambassador in Paris told his employers that the Bishop's tale of a marriage brought about 'by destiny' had been rejected by the Queen-Mother of France and her son Charles IX.

It was wrong, said their majesties, to attribute to force results which were openly brought about 'by free will and premeditated determination'. Mary's confessor, the French Dominican Father Roche Mamerot, appalled by her bigamous marriage, left her and returned to France.

All over Catholic Europe the marriage, rather than the suspicion that Mary had been a party to the murder of her husband, was the decisive factor in destroying her reputation and blighting the hopes of those who saw in her a future Catholic sovereign of England. The Pope said he did not know which of the two was worse, Mary or Elizabeth. He broke off relations, political and financial, with the Queen of Scots.

As for the people of Scotland, the May marriage in Holyrood added the keystone to the arch of suspicions. Their reasoning proceeded on direct and simple lines:

Bothwell was the man most deeply tainted with the suspicion of having murdered Darnley. Knowing this suspicion, the Queen had married him. A packed court had found him free of blame. A feigned rape had been used as the pretext for a false marriage. Bothwell's wife had been freed from her marriage on the grounds of adultery which she had already condoned. And, since Bothwell was still legally married in the eyes of his Catholic sovereign, a consistory court, resuscitated for the purpose from the wreckage of the old Catholic system, found that he had never been married at all!

The people of Scottish burghs like Edinburgh were not sophisticated. They were not fully informed. But they were quite capable of pursuing an argument to its logical conclusion and, if they found it hard to thread the maze of events, there were plenty of guides at hand willing to help them.

Reasoning backwards step by step from the marriage to the murder, they concluded that Mary had consented to Darnley's assassination. Whatever may be said about this verdict, there can be no doubt who had done most to bring it about. Mary was the chief architect of her own ruin.

How to account for a suicidal impulse—a death-wish—so powerful and determined that it prevailed over self-interest, self-respect, policy and religion?

The answer which Mary herself gave and which most people

believed in 1567 is still the most plausible: Prudence and reason were swept away by a cataract of human passion.

She came of a family with no skill in reckoning costs. Her grandfather had thrown away his life and his army on a crazy whim. Her grandson went to the scaffold through an obstinate failure to distinguish rights from realities. In her case, the rock on which the barque foundered was a man, uncouth and brutal, wild and greedy, at once jealous and unfaithful, a rakish adventurer without even looks to commend him.

In the days that followed her wedding, the Queen of Scots had occasion to repent her choice more than once. There is no sign, however, that her storms of revulsion—when she wept and called for death to release her—passed into a settled attitude of regret. There are many signs that point in another direction.

In Edinburgh, in spite of new laws discouraging sedition, broadsheet poems were found. In one Mary was compared with Delilah, Jezebel and Clytemnestra. She was accused of listening, on the night of February 10, for a shot that would announce her husband's murder.

In the early days of June the cloud-heads of rebellion, which had been growing on the horizon, filled the whole sky. Insurgent nobles led by the Earls of Morton and Home, occupied Edinburgh and, at its Cross, called on the lieges to deliver the Queen and revenge Darnley. The response to the summons was poor.

The insurgents were active in propaganda. One of their most effective posters showed the Queen naked to the waist, as a mermaid.[1] Beneath this was the drawing of a hare, as a symbol of Bothwell and, probably, of lust.

Mary and her husband had by this time withdrawn from Holyrood to Borthwick Castle, a stronghold twelve miles east of the town. They were accompanied by regular troops and artillery. Leaving the castle well garrisoned and Mary within its walls,

1. The word had an offensive significance: a siren or wanton. Shakespeare used it of Mary in *A Midsummer Night's Dream*:

> 'Since once I sat upon a promontory,
> And heard a mermaid on a dolphin's back
> Uttering such dulcet and harmonious breath
> That the rude sea grew civil at her song
> And certain stars shot madly from their spheres.'

Bothwell made off to the Border, where he expected an armed force to meet him. Nobody appeared at the place of assembly.

Returning to Borthwick, he was surrounded there by the confederate lords, but escaped after dark. He reached the coastal fortress of Dunbar where, two days later, his wife joined him at three o'clock in the morning. Mary wore male clothes for the night journey. In that guise she attracted less attention. But, in truth, Mary, like many self-dramatising women, had a propensity for transvestism, and the figure to carry it off.

She and her husband marched on Edinburgh at the head of 2000 men or thereabouts—Borderers for the most part, with some Lothian men provided by local lairds, who like Black Ormiston, were in Bothwell's obedience. By this time, Mary had changed into more conventional attire—a short scarlet petticoat she had borrowed in Dunbar, a velvet hat and a scarf.

The rebel army consisted of the horsemen of Morton and Home, Tullibardine and Kerr of Cessford, with foot marching under the orders of nobles like Atholl and Sempill (both Catholics), Ruthven, Glencairn and Lindsay (Protestants).

Bothwell had slightly the edge on his adversaries in numbers, but they enjoyed two notable advantages. In their ranks was that distinguished soldier Kirkcaldy of Grange. And over them floated a white banner with a crude but powerful picture. The dead body of Darnley lay under a tree. Beside him knelt an infant, his son, from whose mouth came the words, 'Judge and revenge my cause, O Lord'. Before the day was over, the message had exerted a baneful influence on morale in the Queen's army.

The two forces met at Carberry Hill a few miles to the east of Edinburgh. But there was no battle. Instead, the French ambassador, Philibert du Croc, intervened.

Speaking first to the rebels, he obtained their conditions for peace: If Mary separated herself from Bothwell, they would be her dutiful servants. As for the question of guilt for the murder of the King, let it be settled by single combat between the lines of the two armies, Bothwell against their champion.

The ambassador carried the news to Mary who told him coolly that the same noblemen who now asked her to leave her husband had signed a bond six weeks earlier begging her to marry him. Bothwell rode up just then and exchanged salutes with the

Frenchman. He said that his enemies were merely envious of the favour he enjoyed: 'But Fortune is free to any who can win her. There is not a man of them but wishes himself in my place!'

Seeing that Mary was in tears he proposed that, to save her more distress, du Croc should ask the insurgents if they had a man of good family ready to step out between the armies. Mary would have no such solution.

By this time the rebel army was on the move. Bothwell invited the ambassador to take up a position commanding a good view: 'You will have more pleasure than ever before, for you will see a fight well fought.'

Du Croc could not help admiring Bothwell's spirit: 'He could not count on half of his men and yet was not dismayed. He had not on his side a single lord of note. I rated his chances higher because he was in sole command.' Du Croc rode back to the rebels who, taking their steel caps in their hands, told him to let them manage the battle in their own way. By this time the afternoon sun was shining in the face of Mary's army. Time, idleness, and that damning banner carried by the rebels were all at work to dispirit them.

Bothwell mounted his charger and sent a herald to challenge his accusers to single combat. James Murray of Purdovis accepted. Mary said, No: Murray was a traitor and of meaner birth than her husband. Accordingly, Bothwell sent his challenge to the nobleman of highest rank on the other side, the Earl of Morton. The Earl accepted, chose the broadsword as his weapon—and asked his friend Lord Lindsay to fight in his name. Lindsay buckled on the two-handed sword of that grim out-facer of kings, Archibald Douglas, Earl of Angus, Bell-the-Cat. It was a hallowed relic in the Douglas family and this was its last public appearance. Twenty gentlemen from either side had now to fix the conditions of the duel.

But while the seconds talked and Bothwell pranced about on his war-horse, it became apparent that there was going to be neither a duel nor a battle. The wind of courage went out of Bothwell's army a little faster than out of the confederates. Grange, chosen to represent his side in a parley, offered the Queen a safe-conduct provided she sent her husband away. Bothwell would be allowed to leave the field unpursued. Mary agreed and with tears and entreaties overcame her husband's doubts.

Her love and Bothwell's may have been stained by folly and worse, it may have prospered through crime but now, at the moment of calamity, it shone with a tragic dignity. In the sight of 5000 men armed for war if not ready for battle, the two ruinous lovers parted with tears and many embraces on that hill above the Esk river.

Bothwell, with thirty horsemen in attendance, rode off to Dunbar; the Queen joined her rebels.

Among them, Lethington, her Secretary of State and, certainly, one with foreknowledge of Darnley's murder, pulled down his hat and pretended not to see his sovereign. Atholl let the Queen know that he was not with the insurgents. Guarded by Captain Lambie's company of professional soldiers, Mary rode towards Edinburgh. At the head of the procession went the banner of the dead King and the praying child.

No doubt the noblemen who had won so complete and bloodless a victory sincerely intended to carry out the terms of their bargain with the Queen. No doubt they were disconcerted by the ugly sequel to Grange's parley. But they were unable to control events as they might have liked.

A new actor now appeared on the stage, unchivalrous, angry and cruel: the commons of Edinburgh, the market women, the shop-keepers, the little craftsmen. They knew nothing of the protocol of war, negotiations and compromise. They knew only what they had been told by propaganda and what they had heard by rumour in the closes and wynds of the town.

They saw on the white banner what they believed to be the truth. They saw, riding among the musketeers in the short red petticoat of a shopkeeper's wife, her eyes red with weeping, her face white, her lips hard, a young woman whose beauty made her offence all the more credible and all the more detestable, a woman whom they believed to have earned the name they spat at her, whom they believed to deserve the penalty they demanded: 'Burn her! Burn the whore! Burn the murderess!'

All the way to Lord Provost Preston's house on the north side of High Street near the Cross, the menacing, hateful chorus pressed on the woman's ears as the crowd pressed forward to reach her horse. The people of Edinburgh, urged on by preachings and prayings, by placards and whispers, had become a revolutionary mob.

More than once during that night Mary came to the window of the Provost's house before which the sinister banner of the rebellion floated. Her hair about her ears, her dress undone, she called out piteously to the crowd that she was kept a prisoner by her own subjects who had betrayed her.

She saw Lethington in the crowd and would not let him pass without speaking to him. Why had she been torn from her husband? The secretary told her that Bothwell was not at all the man she thought him: he had assured Lady Bothwell—with whom he had slept several times since his divorce—that she was his real wife and the Queen only his concubine.

Whatever truth may be in this story, Mary would have none of it. All she asked was to be put in a ship with Bothwell to go where the winds might take them.

When a woman in the crowd shouted insults at her, Mary, true to her nature, swore that she would burn down the town and put out the flames with the blood of its people. Here, surely, was 'the violence of the Lorraine breed' breaking through the shell of domestication.

Riding one on each side of the Queen through the Edinburgh streets, the Earls of Morton and Atholl may well have reflected that they had a wild cat by the tail. What were they to do with this beautiful young virago who was their anointed queen? Send her to France, as the French ambassador proposed? Send her son there too, so that he might be brought up to be as French as his mother? But there was a danger that one day they might find her again among them, with a few thousand French musketeers at her back. And the baby Prince would not only be brought up as a Frenchman, he would inevitably be brought up as a Catholic.

While the lords pondered the problem, their followers scoured Edinburgh for likely murderers of Darnley. They did not labour in vain. Among other suspects, they pulled in Captain William Blackadder, who had been drinking in Katy's Tam's on the night of the explosion and was seen in the street near Blackfriars' Wynd soon afterwards.

Blackadder had appeared in court a few months earlier as an aggrieved person seeking justice. He complained that six Leith fishermen had attacked him and mutilated his servant. When the six found sureties for their reappearance in court they were allowed to go to the herring fishing in Loch Broom.

If the outcome of his case seemed unduly lenient to Blackadder, he had quite different grounds to complain of the treatment now given to him as a suspect. His story was that he had been innocently drinking when he heard the explosion and, through natural curiosity, went outside. However, it was a bad moment for a known dependent of Lord Bothwell's to be visible in the streets. Blackadder was convicted of being art and part of the murder and was executed, protesting his innocence.

It seems likely that the Captain was, in fact, innocent. But he was one of those who might have had a hand in the business. The Captain paid a heavy price for keeping wild company.

More fortunate was Captain James Cullen, one of those roaming mercenary soldiers that Scotland produced by the hundred. He had been in the Danish service and had been given command of a company of the Queen's bodyguard after Riccio's murder. Now he was arrested and kept in irons for a time, then released, and went back to soldiering.

Bastien Pages, whose wedding feast had brought the Queen from Kirk o' Field to Holyrood, was laid by the heels as a suspect. After a spell in the Tolbooth, he too was set at liberty.

While these police activities went on in the town, the ruling junta decided that Mary must, with all speed, be removed and put in safer custody. It may be—the story is told without proof—that from her room in Provost Preston's house, she wrote a letter to Bothwell, 'her dear heart whom she should never forget or abandon', and that this missive was betrayed to her gaolers. Certain it is that she remained then, as in the days of triumph, unshaken in her love for the man she regarded as her husband.

The lords in council decreed on the day after they brought her to Edinburgh that she should be detained in the house and place of Lochleven. They had found her not only reluctant to order the punishment of Bothwell but seeming to fortify and maintain the said Earl Bothwell and his complices in their wicked crimes. Lochleven Castle is built on a small island in the loch of that name in Kinross, about thirty miles by land and water north of Edinburgh. To it the Queen was taken, by night with all speed.

Morton and his friends did not dare to keep her in Edinburgh one day longer. There were several misfortunes that might have befallen. The mob in its frenzy might have broken through the cordon of arquebusiers round the Provost's house and burned the Queen as a faithless and murderous wife. Or, by one of those unpredictable changes of mood to which crowds are susceptible, it might suddenly have veered in her favour.

Or a rival party of the nobility, made up from men like the Duke of Chatelherault, Argyll, Huntly and Cassillis, might have summoned the strength and resolution to rescue her. Or Bothwell, in his stronghold of Dunbar Castle, and by no means a broken man, might have raised the Borders and marched on the town.

For not a few reasons, it was desirable to move the Queen to a remoter and safer place, separated by some miles of sea from her dangerous husband.

12   *Geordie Dalgleish is run to earth*

THE GENERAL BELIEF WAS that Mary was guilty of complicity in Darnley's assassination. This opinion was held by ordinary men and women in Scotland, by lords of both religions, by the French Court, among Spanish diplomats and in official circles in Westminster.

Queen Elizabeth alone seems to have refused to be swept away by the universal wave condemning her cousin. But then Elizabeth had a strong personal antipathy to the prospect of a neighbouring princess, a relation, being found guilty of an odious crime for which burning was the penalty.

Out of common sense or cynicism, through the gossip of the streets, or because her conduct since the murder could only be explained thus, people believed that the Queen of Scots was a murderess. There was no documentary evidence on the matter.

But three days after Mary was taken, a prisoner, to Lochleven, there was a new development. The castle of Edinburgh was held by a garrison commanded by that subtle lawyer-clergyman Sir James Balfour. His guns commanded the town.

Bothwell, trusting a man as deeply involved as himself in the Darnley plot, had installed him there. With an ingratitude which Machiavelli would have admired, Balfour had denied the shelter of the castle—all but impregnable—to the Queen and Bothwell when the nobles rose against them. It was not Balfour's last act of treachery.

On Thursday, June 19, 1567, the Earl of Morton was dining in Edinburgh in the company of Secretary Lethington when 'a certain man' brought him private intelligence:

Three servants of Bothwell's had arrived in the town and passed into the castle. They were Thomas Hepburn, the parson of

Auldhamstocks, John Cockburn, whose brother was the Laird of Skirling, and Geordie Dalgleish, Bothwell's valet.

On hearing the news, which probably reached him with Sir James Balfour's connivance, Morton behaved with exemplary alacrity. Mustering his cousins, Archibald and Robert Douglas and a gentleman named James Johnston of Westerrow, along with other retainers to the number of sixteen or so, he dispatched them to the Castle to search for the three Bothwell men and put them under arrest. The pursuers arrived too late. The covey had flown and separated.

The Douglas party did likewise. One group, led by Archibald Douglas, went after the parson. They found only his horse. James Johnston's party caught up with John Cockburn. Robert Douglas was about to give up the search for Geordie Dalgleish when 'a good fellow' promised, 'for a piece of money', to tell him where to look. The money passed and the unknown Judas earned it.

In the Potterrow, immediately outside the wall of the town a few yards from Kirk o' Field, Geordie was run to earth. In his possession were some legal documents relating to Bothwell's properties. These were brought to Morton.

Dalgleish was then asked by the lords of the privy council, whom Morton had convened, what business had taken him to the Castle, and what he had found there. He replied that he had gone to see about some of his master's clothes and brought nothing away apart from the documents that had been found in his lodging in the Potterrow.

The noblemen were unconvinced by this answer. They decided that Dalgleish should be kept in custody that night and, in the morning, taken to the Tolbooth and put to the torture. The matter was obviously too grave for ordinary humane considerations to be given any weight.

It turned out, however, that the mere sight of the instruments of torment was enough to loosen Geordie's tongue. He led Robert Douglas back to his room in the Potterrow and there, from under the foot of a bed, pulled out a locked silver-gilt box which, he said, he had taken from the castle the day before. This was the famous 'casket'.

It came into Morton's hands at eight o'clock that night. Next morning, in the presence of nine witnesses he had the casket forced open. There were six peers there, in addition to himself. They were evenly divided so far as religion was concerned. Atholl, Sempill and Home were Catholics; Mar, Glencairn and Crichton of Sanquhar were Protestants.

In addition to the peers, the Master of Graham, the Laird of Tullibardine and Secretary Lethington were in the room in Edinburgh when the casket was opened. Inside were found some letters, contracts and sonnets which were 'sighted' (i.e. examined) and immediately afterwards handed back into Morton's keeping. He kept them, he swore,—this narrative is based on Morton's report to an Anglo-Scottish commission eighteen months later—'without alteration, changing, eking or diminishing of anything found in the said box'.

Meanwhile, the public demanded that Mary Stuart should be tried and executed. 'The women be most furious and impudent against the Queen and yet the men be mad enough.' So Queen Elizabeth's ambassador, Sir Nicholas Throckmorton, reported.

The pulpit of St. Giles' Church in Edinburgh shook with the bloodthirsty indignation of John Knox who had hurried back to put his talent for vituperation at the service of the cause. Not long before, he had written in fine prophetic rage: 'Then shall God utterly destroy that hoor in her hoordom, or else He shall put it into the hearts of a multitude to take the same vengeance upon her that was taken of Jezebel and Athaliah; for greater abomination was never in the nature of any woman than is in her.'

Now what Knox had foreseen had come about. The hearts of the multitude were uplifted in holy and vengeful fury. Why, they demanded, should a queen, stained with the crimes of adultery and murder, be treated more leniently than any other guilty woman? There was the court. There was the place of execution. There were the stake and the faggots!

The nobles could, indeed, see pressing reasons why those of gentle —to say nothing of royal—blood should have privileges denied to the commons, but they were in a dilemma. They held the Queen in their grasp. They had lost control of events.

It was useless for the Hamiltons to suggest that, if only Bothwell could be done away with, Mary could marry one of their name. Useless for Argyll to suggest that Mary should marry his brother.

Useless for the French envoy to propose that Mary should be exiled to France and shut up in a convent there.

France had no say in Scottish affairs any longer and lacked the means to acquire one. She had enough troubles of her own. When the Duke of Chatelherault called on the French King he was told roughly to go home and help his sovereign.

The Vicomte de Martiguey, married to one of Mary Stuart's dearest friends in France, swore to rescue her from Lochleven if he were given 3000 arquebusiers for three months, or never set foot in France again. Catherine de' Medici told him he would be better advised to go back to his own administration rather than indulge in such talk. The Constable, Anne de Montmorency, agreed heartily: 'Ho, ho! Is this the time to go into that business again?'

There was, however, a cheaper way in which the task of retrieving the fragments of French diplomacy might be attempted. The Earl of Moray, at that time a visitor to France, might be tempted, by the Order of St. Michael, the captaincy of the Scottish Archers and other rewards, to become the agent of French policy in Scotland. Moray rejected the bait.

But English anxieties over French intentions in Scotland were not completely appeased. 'Have an eye that no French ships steal thither' (to Scotland) 'to convey the Prince away', wrote a correspondent from France to the Earl of Leicester.

The Queen of England, for all her money, threats and diplomacy, had scarcely any more influence than the French over the course of the drama in Scotland. Throckmorton's orders from his sovereign were succinct: Elizabeth, in spite of her grief over Mary's marriage with 'a defamed person', was prepared to restore her to liberty, punish Darnley's assassins and keep the young Prince safe in England. But the lords refused to allow the Englishman to visit the Queen at Lochleven: 'The day being destined, as I did see, to the Communion, continual preaching and common prayer, they could not be absent nor attend to matters of this world'.

Throckmorton reported to London that the temper of the people was so dangerous that 'a stranger over-busy may soon be made a sacrifice among them'. The nobles were forced to make concessions to the fury of the commons. Speaking charitably of Mary in private, they violently demanded her death in public.

When Elizabeth persisted in her demands that Mary be set free,

Throckmorton warned his queen of the danger that the lords would turn towards France. They insisted that Mary must abdicate; the baby Prince must be crowned. As for delivering him to England—never! Unless, of course, he was guaranteed the succession to the English throne.

On July 26, Patrick, Lord Lindsay of the Byres, brought the ultimate sanction to bear on the captive at Lochleven. She knew him well. One encounter with Lindsay she would never forget. On the night Riccio was killed, Mary had 'felt his cold dagger pass by her cheek'. Now the murderer came to offer a brutal choice: she must abdicate or be executed.

The blackmail was successful. Mary lay in bed after a miscarriage of twins. She was in no state to resist the threat that Lindsay held over her. Mary signed an act of abdication and a document which set up a regency. She comforted herself with the thought that what was extorted by force or menace could not be sustained in law.

About noon next day, the Lords, booted and spurred, called on Throckmorton in his lodging in Edinburgh and invited him to attend the coronation of the Prince at Stirling. He refused, adding that the Prince would need a council. With a loud murmuring they retorted, 'Either the Queen is advised by the worst council or by no council. My lord, we will trouble you no longer. The day passeth away and we have far to ride.' And took their leave.

Sir Nicholas was in a disagreeable situation. His alarming mistress showered on him the sternest admonitions: 'Tell them that we will revenge their sovereign. Quote St. Paul in Romans: "The head is not subject to the foot." '

Throckmorton, afraid for Mary's life, was not too happy about his own. 'I am in a town guarded by men of war,' he complained. 'I have no horses, but must depend on these lords' orders for the furthering of me and my train. I cannot depart but at their pleasure.' He asked permission to return to Berwick. A month passed before Elizabeth allowed her anxious ambassador to leave his post.

At the age of twenty-five Mary ceased to be Queen of Scotland; at the age of thirteen months her son James became its king. John Knox, whatever misgivings he may have had about the sinful leniency shown to Mary Stuart, preached the coronation sermon at Stirling, finding his text in the Book of Kings, where Joas was crowned, very young. Lindsay took his oath in the church that Mary had given up her throne willingly.

Later on he was asked to go to England to give the same testimony. But on that occasion, 'My lord,' he cried, 'if you cause me to go to England with you, I will spill the whole matter.'

Mary's half-brother, the Earl of Moray, returning to Scotland from his well-timed travels abroad, became Regent. On his way through London he told the Spanish ambassador, Guzman de Silva, that his sister's knowledge of the murder plot against Darnley was proved beyond doubt by a letter she had written to Bothwell in her own hand on three sheets of paper.

In this, she had urged Bothwell not to delay putting into execution what he had arranged because her husband used such fair words to win her round that she might be moved by them. She said that she would stop at a house on the road (presumably from Glasgow) and try to give him 'a draught'. If this could not be done she would take him to Kirk o' Field. On the night of the murder, she had petted and fondled her husband—that had been the worst thing of all!

This conversation in London occurred about six weeks after the opening of the 'casket'. Much has been made of the discrepancies between the 'letter' described by Moray and Casket Letter II. These discrepancies are, however, no more than might reasonably exist between an actual text and an account of it at second-hand by Moray and at third-hand by Guzman de Silva.

What makes an impression is Moray's moral revulsion from his sister's guilt, in which he sincerely believed. He was appalled by the petting and the fondling of the doomed man. It was his sister who was charged with this treachery—and Moray recoiled, not only as one who was as stiff a moralist as any in Europe, but also as a Stewart grieved, as he said, 'for the honour of his father's house', and—although he did not say so—all the more sensitive because he was himself a bastard of that house.

When he arrived in Edinburgh he found additional reasons for dismay. Scotland was lurching into anarchy, and his sister's life was in greater danger than ever. The pulpits still bellowed for blood. The Protestant mob, responding sensitively as always to events in Europe which affected the Religion, were aware of a sinister happening.

The Duke of Alva's Spanish army had arrived in Brussels. The

Spanish Terror began in Flanders. To the furthest limits of the Protestant world, tremors of alarm were carried, bringing bitterness and fanaticism with them.

There was, too, a change in the local situation which adversely influenced Mary's cause. The Hamiltons, who for reasons of their own had been Mary's supporters, offered to join the victorious confederates. Their conditions, as stated by those consecrated rascals, the Archbishop of St. Andrews and the Abbot of Kilwinning, both of whom were Hamiltons, were that Mary should be executed and that Darnley's brother, representative of the Lennox line, should be excluded from the succession to the throne.

So long as Mary lived, she might escape and avenge herself on her enemies. In the forfeiture of estates that would follow her restoration, who would suffer most? The greatest landowners, Huntly, Argyll, the Hamiltons. Besides, if she lived, she might have more children. Whereas at present, as the Laird of Tullibardine put it delicately to Throckmorton, 'they account but the little king betwixt them and home'. And the little King might die . . . Tullibardine spoke with feeling: his sister, the Countess of Mar, was King James's governess.

Vicious, faithless, incapable, handsome—so were the Hamiltons as Throckmorton saw them. His contempt for them was even sharper than that which Charles IX had shown to the head of the clan, the Duke of Chatelherault, in Paris only a fortnight earlier.

On his arrival in Edinburgh, Moray took command of the situation. Four days later, he visited his sister in her island prison. He found her in excellent health and spoke to her, at first in obscure phrases, then more bluntly in an interview after supper which lasted until one in the morning and was renewed next day. What did they talk of, that strange pair?

'Her misgovernment and all such disorders as might touch her conscience, her honour or surety.' He spoke, so it was rumoured, rather like a confessor than an adviser. She wept bitterly, acknowledging that she had made mistakes.

He told her that her life would be in peril if she incited England or France to molest the country, or if she persisted in her inordinate affection for Bothwell. If she wished to be saved, she must show that she detested her former life; the murder of her husband; Bothwell.

 • After a new fit of weeping, she kissed him 'very lovingly'. With
 ⁓ that they parted.

Moray's purpose may have been to gain time so that public
feeling might simmer down and some reliable proof be given that
his sister had recovered from the fever of Bothwell. Perhaps some
new, respectable marriage could in the end be found for her. . . .
In the meantime, she must remain in her pleasant incarceration
on the lake although the Queen of England threatened to make
war to release her, although the mob threatened to drag her to a
scaffold and although Mary herself . . .

The Queen of Scots had no sense of guilt, only a fleeting grasp of
realities, but a blazing awareness of her rights.

One day late in August, Throckmorton made his last appeal to
the confederate lords to release their queen, adding the threats
which Elizabeth had commanded him to deliver. The appeal was
rejected in language which was Lethington's and lacks neither spirit
nor vivacity:

So far from meaning any harm to Queen Mary, the lords wished
she were queen of all the world. Unfortunately, she was, just then,
to be treated as a person with a burning fever whose desires must on
no account be granted. When her passion moderated, she would
have nothing but good from them. As for Elizabeth's threats, 'You
must think, my lord ambassador, your wars are not unknown to us.
You will burn our Borders, and we will do the like to yours, and
whensoever you invade us, we are sure France will aid us, for their
league standeth fast.'

After giving his royal mistress a brilliant account of the conference, there was nothing for Throckmorton to do but make his way
to Berwick, which he did, with infinite thankfulness, declining a
parting gift of gilt plate from the Scotsmen.

Eight months after the breakdown of the English attempts at
rescue, on May 1, Mary sent a letter from her prison to Catherine de'
Medici, begging for help, for troops, complaining in pitiful
language of the closeness with which she was guarded—'I have no
leisure but while they dine, or when they sleep, for their girls sleep
with me'. The letter ends with a broken sentence. Suddenly, Mary
wrote no further; suddenly, she decided to hand the letter over,
unfinished, to the bearer. Mary's imprisonment had not been so

strict, her captivity not so helpless, as she pretended. The time for writing was past.

Next day at supper time, she was rowed to the further shore by George Douglas, the young brother of her gaoler, whom she had captivated. All the gates of the castle were locked on the outside and the boats left behind had been made unserviceable.

Alexander Hepburn of Riccarton, a cousin of Bothwell's, was waiting for them with ten horses; two miles further on, Lord Seton met them, with thirty horsemen. Crossing the Firth of Forth by the ferry, Mary paused at Niddry long enough to instruct the Laird of Riccarton to seize Dunbar Castle and send news of her escape to Bothwell.

Seven months before, Mary's lover, escaping from the victorious faction in Scotland with two ships and 140 followers, had arrived in the Norwegian harbour of Bergen. By the time Mary escaped from Loch Leven, Bothwell was in a Danish prison.

Riccarton failed to take Dunbar Castle and, probably, did not reach Bothwell with Mary's message.

Mary rode on towards the west. Picking up armed support on the way, she arrived at length in Hamilton, a village on the river Clyde some miles above Glasgow. The Hamilton family had decided their interests would be best served by taking Mary's side.

But the escape that had begun so brilliantly came to an early and dismal end. Moray, attending an assize in Glasgow, called on the lieges to join him there with provisions for fifteen days. Maybe 3000 obeyed him, a disappointing muster, only about half as many as rallied round his sister. When the two forces met at Langside outside Glasgow, Moray's army was handled with the greater skill. It appeared, too, that the Hamiltons and their associates had no enthusiasm for the fight. After quarter of an hour's half-hearted work with spears they broke and ran. Riding south ninety miles before resting, Mary reached Dundrennan on the shores of Solway Firth. From there she sent Elizabeth a letter: 'I have no hope but in your goodness'—and the heart-shaped diamond which Elizabeth had once given her.

Next day, rejecting the advice of her Catholic companions that she should take ship for France, the Queen of Scotland, Dowager of France, stood on English soil.

She was destitute, defeated, defiant, and, as it seemed, impenitent.

Her woes were obvious and she made much of them. She wrote to her uncle, the Cardinal of Lorraine, about 'injuries, calumnies, imprisonment, famine, cold, heat, flight—and then I had to sleep upon the ground, and drink sour milk, and eat oatmeal without bread, and been three nights like the owls, without a female in this country'. It had been a dreadful experience yet not, surely, or her words have done her wrong, merely dreadful.

This was the young woman who had gone to war merrily against Huntly, against her brother, Moray, who had bemused Darnley into abetting her escape from Holyrood and George Douglas into freeing her from Lochleven, who had, above all, bedazzled Darnley into making the journey to Kirk o' Field where he met his death.

She had loved Bothwell—she loved him still at that moment when she did not know precisely where he was—somewhere in the north, in the grey mists, beyond the grey seas, hunted as she was hunted, reckless as she was reckless, daring as she loved men to be daring. 'She delighteth much to hear of hardiness and valiance,' said one who met her then, 'commending by name all approved hardy men of her country.'

Is there not, in the catalogue of miseries which she addressed to her Uncle Charles, an undertone of achievement, a subdued cry of exaltation? She was not wise, like Elizabeth, nor patient, like Catherine de' Medici. She could dissimulate; she could play a part as well as either of those great political actresses; but she could not wait nor scheme; she was handicapped, as they were not, by blinding surges of passion. She lacked the sense of proportion, of measure, which the other two possessed, deriving it in one case from an endangered childhood, in the other from early widowhood in a strange land. In contrast with them, Mary Stuart had been brought up as the pampered daughter of two royal houses.

She had, however, a gift which came to her in moments of desperate crisis: she could call up extraordinary resources of sexual magnetism, concentrate them and launch them with instinctive mastery and overwhelming power so that, within hours, the tables were turned on her triumphant enemies.

The gift did not desert her now. Before many hours had passed, the poor refugee in England was weaving her spells once more, as ruthless and indomitable as ever. Her first victim was the first important English official she met. Elizabeth's Vice-Chamberlain, Sir Francis Knollys.

He observed the ease of her manner, her eagerness to renew the fight, her desire for vengeance. Soon he was captivated by the dangerous and beautiful waif whom the storm of the world had blown to the Solway shore, by her eloquence, her 'discreet head' and the stout courage which made pain and perils seem pleasant for victory's sake. 'What,' he asked in honest bewilderment and admiration, 'is to be done with such a lady, such a princess?'

It was eighteen years before his mistress the Queen gave her answer to that question.

13 *Eight letters in a casket*

By the time mary reached England, five of the Kirk o' Field conspirators had made their depositions and paid the penalty at the Mercat Cross of Edinburgh for 'the most cruel, shameful, treasonable and abominable slaughter and murder of umquhile the King's grace'. The small fry, Powrie and Geordie Dalgleish, were first to go, in July 1567. Hay of Tala had followed them in September, and Hepburn of Bowton in January.

For the sum of £4 2s. John Brown, messenger, and a boy took portions of the dismembered corpses to be displayed on the gates of Glasgow, Hamilton, Dumbarton, Ayr and Wigtown. Four other boys earned £3 17s. by taking limbs so that other Scottish burghs might have the same warning of the consequences of crime. On creels and packing for the relics 10s. was spent.

However, others in the plot were still at large. French Paris seems to have gone to Denmark with his master. There he was laid by the heels and shipped back to Scotland in August 1569. No time was lost in stringing him up. Pat Wilson disappeared and was never heard of again.

Lord Bothwell himself, the arch-villain, was living in reasonable comfort in a Danish prison, and King Frederick was much exercised in mind what to do with his captive. Send him back to Scotland to the scaffold that was ready for him? Accept the courteous offer of the Scottish Regent, Moray, who had sent over Colonel Clerk, a Scottish mercenary in Danish pay, to execute him on the spot?

King Frederick called in four dukes, relatives of his, and the Elector of Saxony to advise him where his duty lay. After profound cogitation, they found (the Elector of Saxony demurring) that Bothwell should not be sent back to Scotland.

That leaves the two Ormistons, the Black Laird and his uncle

Rob, who were lurking in Liddesdale in the Border country, in the Laird of Whithaugh's house. There they had, as their companion, the Laird's prisoner, Ker of Fawdonside, a brutal murderer of Riccio. It was reported, too (again by a hostile source) that the two Ormistons visited Mary secretly while she was in Carlisle.

In that case, the Queen would have given audience to two men wanted for the murder of her late husband, Darnley. But this would not be wholly surprising, for she had knighted one of them at a time when she knew well he was believed to be one of the murderers.

The group that blew up Kirk o' Field was not, after all, recruited by Bothwell from obscure corners of the country. Its leaders were well-known figures at Court, gentlemen of rank although not noblemen, accustomed to talk on easy terms with the Queen. Young Tala, on his way to execution, blamed his fall from grace upon the corrupting influence of the Court which had, he said, turned his mind from reading the Bible. The Kirk o' Field outrage was carried out by men Mary Stuart saw every day of her life. Did they commit the crime against her will? Did they take her approval for granted? Was she completely ignorant of what was going to happen, or was she deceived about the nature of the enterprise? Did she never have the curiosity to ask any of them what he had been doing between the hours of ten and two in the morning on Sunday, February 9?

After he was tried and sentenced to death in December 1573 Ormiston made a confession in Edinburgh Castle to John Brand, minister of the Canongate Kirk, a man of the highest character. Ormiston said that he had never spoken to the Queen about the murder nor she to him. But when the rumour spread that he had been present at the killing, he took the matter to the Queen, who shrugged her shoulders and said nothing.

If Ormiston was telling the truth—and why should he be lying? —what was the meaning of Mary's conduct on that occasion? Would it not have been natural for her to ask him, 'Is there any substance in the rumour?' But, as she is not known to have enquired into Bothwell's still more serious part in the conspiracy, her silence to Ormiston becomes less puzzling.

What *was* Mary Stuart's share in the murder of her husband? Foreknowledge? Complicity before the event? A guilty acquiescence in it after the event? Or total, deluded innocence? In the end, the answer to the question depends on what sort of woman Mary was and what were her relations with Bothwell.

No questions in all history, perhaps, have been given so many contradictory answers as those concerning Mary Stuart. Even the colour of the Scottish queen's eyes and hair is disputed. The eyes were grey and are sometimes described as brown. Her hair? Blonde, auburn, or black? Various reports exist, confused by the fact that, like other fashionable women of her time, Mary cut her hair and wore perukes. The natural colour of her hair seems to have been something between blonde and chestnut.

She is said by some to have been a frail woman, subject to serious maladies. Yet she rode sixty—even ninety—miles without rest.

One eminent historian (French) believes she was a nymphomaniac; another (Scottish) says she was sexually frigid. Her son was alleged to be, not Darnley's but Riccio's; and, in another version, not her son at all but some other woman's, hers having been still-born.

She was innocent, a martyr, a fit candidate for canonisation. So some have thought. Others, less enthusiastic, have remembered how she defied the opinion of her family, the Guises, rejected the warnings of her confessor and dared the wrath of the Pope in order to make a bigamous marriage with a Protestant. Others again have held her to be a monster of iniquity, tempting susceptible young men to their ruin.

To some extent, the blurring of her image as it has come down in history is due to the intense heat of partisanship round the Queen of Scots. It is necessary, by an effort, to put aside prejudices: personal, in favour of a beautiful woman overwhelmed by misfortune; religious, for or against one who was the symbol of one faith or the enemy of another; above all, the prejudice, created by time, change, the differences of cultural and moral environment, which makes it hard for one age to understand another.

How can men and women of the twentieth century see, clearly and in perspective, their ancestors of the sixteenth? To us they seem a little mad, apparently afflicted with a special form of schizophrenia, which makes them appear attractive, talented, perplexing half-monsters, capable of crimes and ardours of which we know nothing; at once self-consciously pagan and profoundly Christian;

sceptical and bigoted, sensual and austere, erudite and barbarous.

Mary Stuart was brought up in the same nursery as the family of Catherine de' Medici, each of whom carried a double curse of heredity. Both of the grandfathers, François I and Lorenzo de' Medici, died of syphilis. Active still in the blood of the third generation, the enemy picked off its victims one by one until at last, as Michelet says with obvious relish, '*il nous delivra des Valois*'. Consider, one by one, Catherine's appalling brood:

François II, feeble and short-lived, who died, as the Duke of Alva said, 'of Mary Stuart', who died, in medical fact, of inner ear disease; Charles IX, who had an insane craving for blood and fired with an arquebus on his subjects from a window in the Louvre; Henri III, who preferred women's clothes and men's company; and Marguerite de Valois, a nymphomaniac who had an incestuous love affair with her brother, the Duc d'Alençon.

Mary was, for a time, an ornament of the most brilliant and corrupt court in Europe, a new Olympus in which Henri II was Jupiter, his queen was Juno, his mistress was Diana and Ronsard was Apollo. The French palaces were the resorts of artists, sculptors, dancers and prostitutes. Catherine de' Medici, who cleared the professional loose women out, pursued policy by traditional methods when she enrolled her famous Flying Squadron of beautiful, aristocratic girls to spy on and, if possible, to seduce susceptible young men of the Huguenot camp (like the Prince de Condé).

When Jeanne d'Albret, the Calvinist Queen of Navarre, came to Paris in search of a consort for her son, she wrote to him, 'I would not have you live here for the world. I wish you to marry and come out of this corruption with your wife. . . . Here it is not the men who solicit the women, but the women the men.'

In an atmosphere at once beguiling and pernicious, in scenes embellished by the most accomplished artists of the age, the young exile from Scotland became early acquainted with worldly wisdom and worldly folly. Watched over by her Guise relations, she remained unspotted at that fantastic Valois Court, but she would certainly know the nature of the world around her.

When she was pitted against the Scottish nobles, she did not come to the conflict as a hapless amateur matched with ruthless professionals. She had been trained in the same school as they had, in France. But she was outmanœuvred, isolated and disarmed.

In politics, it is not the finest and most brilliant qualities of mind that are decisive. Mary had every gift, it has been said,[1] save moderation and good sense. The lack of them was fatal.

The short explanation of her ruin is Bothwell. She was passionately in love with him and she remained so for too long. Whether he was in love with her or was simply intoxicated by her beauty it is hard to say. He may not have known himself. What is certain is that she did not believe the accusations brought against him, did not quickly give him up and never regretted him. When she swore she would go to the ends of the earth with him in a petticoat she uttered something that she meant and voiced something profound about their relationship.

Instinctively she knew that he was the same sort of human being as she. They were banded together against an enemy world, the Queen divided by religion from her people and the Earl divided by jealousy from his caste. When the conduct of Mary Stuart in 1567 is considered, let it not be forgotten that she was in the grip of an ungovernable and obdurate infatuation.

Over and over again she had but to deny Bothwell, declare that her marriage was no marriage (which would have been true), and her life would no longer be in danger, her crown and liberty would, in all probability, have been restored to her after a term of abeyance. And her love for Bothwell? How readily it would have been explained by supernatural means at a time when magic was taken seriously and Bothwell was, by many people, believed to be a warlock. Not once did she waver in her loyalty to her lover.

The supreme problem about her is, of course, whether she was or was not a party to the murder. It has been argued on her behalf that while she was responsible for luring her husband back to Edinburgh, she had no idea that Bothwell meant to kill him. That she knew some mischance would befall the wretch is plain from a passage in Casket Letter II which is universally acknowledged to be hers: 'I am in doing of a work here that I hate greatly.'

Did this mean no more than that Mary was troubled in conscience because she was deceiving Darnley? He was going to be made a prisoner so as to keep him out of mischief? And nothing more, as far as she was aware. Then Bothwell and his associates blew up

1. By Michelet.

Kirk o' Field and presented the Queen with a *fait accompli*. This reconstruction of events is unconvincing.

There was no reason in the world why Mary, in the early morning of February 10, 1567, should have accepted Bothwell's crime and, in effect, made it her own. Her natural reaction as a wife would be to denounce it. Her instinctive response as a woman would be to shrink from it in horror. Always on the assumption that she was not, in some sense, committed to it. Only if she herself were involved, in consent and will and hatred of Darnley, does her conduct become explicable.

What *was* that conduct? A sham trial of Bothwell and a sham exculpation, a fictitious 'rape', a contrived divorce, and a false marriage. This is the course of behaviour which makes it so hard to believe that Mary had no complicity in the crime. What form that complicity took may be in doubt.

Even in the sixteenth century, the golden age of political assassination,[1] rulers usually left to others the tedious duties of planning and execution. But that there was between Mary and Bothwell an understanding of what was going to happen, a parcelling out of responsibilities between them and a promise of the rewards that success would bring—this, surely, is a likely assumption. For Bothwell the prizes would be rich. They were: A dukedom, a royal marriage, estates, political power second only to that of the Queen.

It is probable that Mary Stuart never felt any guilt for Darnley's death. It was a necessary act in which the moral issues were covered by *raison d'état*, and for which a sovereign was not answerable save to God and her conscience. Queen Elizabeth seems to have felt very much the same about the business: more concerned that her 'good sister' would have enough statesmanship to clear herself of suspicions than with the deeper issues of guilt and innocence.

To one party in the debate, however, these issues were of the highest importance: the Calvinist preachers who seized on them as material of incomparable value for propaganda. It made no difference that Bothwell was a Protestant and Darnley—if anything—a Catholic. The dead man became a slaughtered saint and Bothwell the accomplice of that adulterous Jezebel, Mary Stuart. The propaganda called into being something that never existed in Scotland

1. Mary's Guise uncle François and two of her Guise cousins, Henri and Louis, were victims.

before and which certainly the Queen had not reckoned on, an organised and effective public opinion. It limited the power to manœuvre and compromise of the nobles who overthrew the Queen; it alarmed Elizabeth; and it deprived Mary's armies of the will to fight. Knox had the insight to perceive and the eloquence to exploit the opportunity that had been given him. The final victory was his.

Puzzling and fascinating, the Casket Letters have won more attention from the historians than perhaps they deserve. They had little influence on the events that led to the downfall of the Queen. At that time they had been seen only by a handful of men and their existence was known only to a few more. What value as evidence for or against Mary can they have today? In the nature of things it can only be secondary.

What we have are copies, and translations at that. They are without signatures; only one of them bears a day and a place of origin, and that was probably added later. How then can they be pronounced with certainty either genuine or forged?

Morton's account of the circumstances of their discovery has the ring of truth, although it may not be the whole truth. They were inspected by ten councillors who knew Mary's handwriting, and it may be assumed the inspection of such interesting and important documents was thorough. However, a year passed before the letters were submitted to an Anglo-Scottish Commission at York. Who is to say that, in the interval, no sly insertion was slipped into the text?

One letter above all (II) is of critical importance, since its contents can hardly have been invented and since it implies foreknowledge by the writer—who can only be Mary—of Bothwell's intention to do some harm to her husband. It has been suggested, therefore, that this letter has been tampered with, 'improved', so that Mary's complicity would be better established.

But to tamper with a document is to destroy it. The 'improver' must substitute a complete new text, carefully forged from start to finish. Would such a forgery, however 'improved' its substance might be, really be more impressive as a piece of evidence than an incontestably original letter, even if it only showed that Mary was writing in confidential terms to Bothwell a week or so before her husband's assassination?

The false article would certainly be more likely than the genuine to be doubted and denounced. Mary herself might insist on seeing it. Moray would certainly inspect it. He believed in his sister's guilt, but would he be a party to fabricating evidence against the head of his family? The reputation of the Stewarts not only touched his honour, it also involved his interest.

There were eight letters in the gilt box, along with a long (bad) poem and two marriage contracts. Using the traditional numbering, once supposed to denote some priority in time:

In Letter I (294 words long in the Scottish translation) the writer chides the recipient for forgetting her; waiting on news of him has given her almost as much joy as his return will—surely, a pleasing conceit. She goes on to say that she will bring 'the man' with her to Craigmillar on Monday. 'He is more gay than ever you saw him . . . you may say he makes love to me.' It has been supposed that 'the man' was Darnley. But General Mahon,[1] followed by M. H. Armstrong Davison[2] has suggested that Mary was here speaking of her infant son. This seems a reasonable suggestion. The letter can then be made to agree with the Queen's journey from Stirling to Craigmillar on Monday, January 13, 1567. In that case, the final note 'From Glasgow this Saturday in the morning' would be either a forgery or a guess by some clerk.

The main body of the letter is unquestionably Mary's and its importance lies in the evidence it gives of her passionate love for Bothwell.

Letter II (3132 words) is the longest and incomparably the most important of the set. Nobody can be surprised that it has aroused a great deal of controversy. It is rambling, repetitious, and fascinating; the text is interrupted by lists of topics made to assist the writer's memory. It is written in Glasgow, and unquestionably the bulk of it is by Mary. Armstrong Davison[3] supposes that two letters, one to Bothwell, the other to Moray, have here been amalgamated and that a few sentences from another woman's letter to Bothwell have been inserted.

Of course, it is possible that tricks were played. But it is hard to see what motive there was in amalgamating two letters when one

1. *Mary Queen of Scots*, p. 111.
2. *The Casket Letters*, p. 110.
3. *The Casket Letters*, p. 128 et seq.

did not materially add to the impression made by the other. The passages supposedly taken from another woman's letter describe— among endearments—how the writer is making a bracelet for her lover. Would such a trifle be worth the trouble of forging?

The Letter is important because in the parts that are indisputably Mary's, it demonstrates that she was knowingly a party to an enterprise against her husband which troubled her conscience.

Letter III (717 words) is written in an elaborate, affected style quite unlike the first two. The writer, complaining of the neglect and faithlessness of her lover, sends him, by Paris, a lock of her hair with a locket which she describes in detail and with some strained and fanciful analogies.

The difference in feeling and style between this Letter and Letters I and II has naturally encouraged the belief that it was written by another woman, probably French, who was, or had been, in love with Bothwell. It may be that this correspondent of Bothwell's wrote, like Mary, in the Italian hand and that the men who inspected the letter believed that they had come upon another epistle of the Queen's. This certainly seems more likely than that there was deliberate forgery of a document which, even if it is credited, does not add much to the case against Queen Mary.

There is one other possibility. Letter III may be a conscious literary exercise with some model in mind. In its extraordinary artifice, does it not suggest this?

Letter IV (534 words) has been thought to refer to the Queen's reported design to promote a duel between Darnley and her brother Lord Robert Stewart. There is, however, no evidence for anything of that kind. One sentence runs, 'I have promised to bring him to him tomorrow'. What it means cannot even be surmised. The greater part of the letter warns Bothwell against the wiles of some other woman.

Armstrong Davison[1] finds the style quite different from that of Mary in Letters I and II and similar to that of Letter III. He assumes therefore that the final sentence is a forgery: 'I durst not write this before Joseph, Bastien and Joachim' (all known to be servants of the Queen) 'that did but depart even when I began to write', and he finds it improbable that a sovereign, even in love, could write a 'fawning paragraph' like this:

1. *The Casket Letters*, p. 171.

'Now, Monsieur, I have already broken my promise, for you have ordered me not to send or write anything, yet I do not do it to offend you and, if you knew the fear which I have of doing so, you would not have so many contrary suspicions which, however, I cherish as proceeding from the thing in the world which I most desire and seek, which is your good grace.'

Yet the sentence, in its humility, resembles Mary's approaches to the Duke of Norfolk a few years later: 'Let me know your mind, and whether you are not offended at me, as I fear you are. I have sought to avoid displeasure for fear of you . . . I will be true and obedient unto you, as I have promised, as long as I live.'

One phrase seems to stamp Letter IV as Mary's: 'As the turtle dove, I shall remain alone to lament the absence.' In this there seems to be a strong echo from a sonnet of Ronsard, Mary's favourite poet:

> 'Que dis-tu, que fais-tu, pensive tourterelle
> Dessus cet arbre sec?—Viateur, je lamente.'

Letter V (277 words) speaks of the folly of some woman who has made Bothwell annoyed with the writer. It has been supposed that this refers to Mary's maid of the bedchamber, Margaret Carwood who married John Stewart of Tullipowreis the day after Darnley's assassination—and perhaps had urgent reason to marry him. The supposition rests on a clerk's endorsement of the French copy.

The letter is marked by an extreme humility of tone ('my obedience, my faithfulness, constancy and voluntary subjection') recalling Letter IV. It opens with a phrase ('My heart, alas') resembling the opening of Letter VI (426 words): 'Alas, my love, why is your trust put in a person so unworthy' etc. It contains an expression characteristic of Mary's style, 'Summa [en somme]¹ he is all against it.' It speaks of the objection of 'your false brother-in-law' who insists 'that with mine honour I could never marry you, seeing that being married you did carry me away' and says that his people would not tolerate the foolish enterprise and that the lords would withdraw their consent. It has been taken for granted that in this passage Mary is speaking of the fraudulent ravishment and marriage.

1. It occurs eight times in the Letters, which total 5864 words.

Now it is suggested[1] that the writer is not Mary at all but 'the unknown woman' and that the real meaning of the French is not that Bothwell had carried her away but that he had brought her to his castle. However, there is no evidence that an unknown woman existed or that she had been brought to live under Bothwell's roof. Why should it be thought dishonourable for her to marry him when, presumably, she had already been living with him?

Again, why should 'the lords' be concerned with any adultery or marriage of Bothwell's, unless that with the Queen? It seems far easier to believe that Letter VI relates to the 'ravishment' and that it was written, as its style suggests, by Mary.

The authorship of Letter VII (230 words) is not for a moment in doubt. Mary is writing to someone who, she says, well deserves a pardon if he advances himself above the duty of a subject 'to make yourself sure of the lords and free to marry'. Can this be anyone but Bothwell?

The excuses which she suggests he should put forward for his presumption—that he wished to strengthen his position as her servant, he 'used a humble request joined to an importunate action —echo those that Mary instructed her ambassador in France to make on Bothwell's behalf to the French Court: 'From the conspiracies of his enemies he could not find himself in surety, without he were assured of our favour to endure without alteration.'

There is a suggestion that the letter was written to George Douglas, a boy of eighteen, youngest brother of the Laird of Lochleven, who helped to deliver Mary from that island prison. But the casket was forced open ten months before the escape.

The letter could not, in that case, have been one of its contents. Nor is it easy to see how, if it were in George Douglas's keeping, it later fell into the hands of Mary's enemies. He was one of the sixteen who accompanied her on the fishing boat to England. He seems to have remained in her service in exile. In 1570 Mary wrote from prison to the King and Queen-Mother of France recommending George Douglas to their favour.

Letter VIII (261 words) is clearly by Mary and is usually supposed to relate to the pretended rape and to the reluctance of the Earl of Sutherland and others to be party to the charade. Mary reports that

1. *The Casket Letters*, p. 188.

she has 300 horse of Huntly's and Livingstone's; she begs Bothwell to take care that he has a larger force.

There is, however, a possibility that the letter was written at the time when the confederates were massing against the Queen and Bothwell. In favour of this opinion is the form in which Huntly is spoken of: 'your brother-in-law that was'. Bothwell was not divorced from Huntly's sister at the time of the 'rape'. On the other hand, Mary speaks of Huntly's fear of being charged with treason, which will be lessened if Bothwell musters a strong force.

Probability seems to point towards the ravishment. But the date of Letter VIII may remain an open question.

The 158 lines of verse found in the casket with the letters have been thought by some to be additional proof of the Queen's guilty love. In spite of the lines

> 'Into his hands and into his full power
> I place my son, my honour and my life,
> My hand, my subjects, my subjected soul',

it has, also, been argued that Mary was not their author.

There are lines which echo the conceits and the language of Letter III, which least resembles the rest of Mary's correspondence. A Frenchwoman, a *précieuse*, abjectly in love with Bothwell, perhaps mother of a son by him—must we look for such a being? Certainly, we shall not find her, but she may have existed for all that. It is strange, though, that she makes no appearance in public. Is it too much of a coincidence that Mary likewise was a Frenchwoman, filled with all the literary conceits of the time, given to extravagances of humility in love? She had a son and she had subjects.

The balance of judgment must be that she wrote those deplorable 'sonnets'.

The contents of the casket, although they are not needed to establish a case for or against the Queen of Scots, have a spell, a mystery of their own. Their later story may be glanced at before they are left to confront the generations with their enigmatic frown.

During the rule of four Scottish regents they were preserved. When Lord Morton was executed in 1580 they came, by secret channels, into the possession of the Earl of Gowrie who resisted all

Queen Elizabeth's attempts to lay hands on them. In 1584 Gowrie was arrested and beheaded. The Casket Letters came into the possession of Mary's son, the eighteen-year-old King James VI.

There can be no doubt at all that this was an opportunity not to be missed by a young man zealous to vindicate his mother's honour. He was called Davy Riccio's son to his face. Here was the moment to prove to the world that his mother was innocent of Darnley's blood. If the Letters showed signs of garbling or forgery, then there would be an immense revulsion in favour of an injured queen, then still alive. All that was needed was that the Letters should be exhibited.

From the moment that they came into the King's hands, they have never been seen.

14 *The key of the cage*

Y EARS PASSED BEFORE THE Kirk o' Field affair was finally allowed to become history.

The Ormistons were sentenced in 1573. One of them made a spectacularly pious end. The Earl of Morton was executed in 1580, admitting his preknowledge of the business. In the following year, John Binning, servant of Archibald Douglas, parson of Glasgow, was hanged for his part in the murder.

Douglas himself, when brought to trial, argued his way out of danger with the help of a jury packed with his relatives. A bribe of £1000 from Queen Elizabeth to King James VI may also have served to stay the hand of retribution.

The evidence against Douglas was slight. A slipper, said to be his, had been found at the scene of the murder. Possibly, however, he had played his part that night. Mrs. Martin and Mrs. Crockett swore they had seen eleven men in the party hurrying into the town from Kirk o' Field after the explosion.

Hepburn of Bowton, in his confession, insisted that only nine men were at the deed. William Powrie spoke of two unidentified men with cloaks about their faces who met him at the entrance to Blackfriars at a time when Hepburn was within the gate. The night was dark and it is possible, then, that Douglas and his servant were hovering on the outskirts of the enterprise without Hepburn being aware of it.

The fates of some eminent figures of the time may be briefly mentioned. The Earl of Moray was assassinated in 1570. Mary, in a spasm of exultation, awarded a pension to the murderer of her half-brother. The Earl of Lennox was killed in 1571. In the same year Archbishop Hamilton was hanged in his vestments. In 1572 John Knox died, in bed. Kirkcaldy of Grange, the soldier whose military talent brought about the downfall of the Queen's cause at Carberry Hill and Langside, was executed in 1573. Maitland of Lethington, the too-subtle secretary, died in prison at the same time. The Earl of Bothwell died, in a Danish prison, insane, in 1578. Morton perished in 1580. Sir James Balfour, that eminent churchman, judge and betrayer who 'had served with all parties, had deserted all yet had profited by all', who had rowed in the convict galleys with Knox, plotted a murder with Bothwell, and taken the field at Langside with Moray, died in 1583, full of years and honours.

Thus, when Mary Stuart went to the block at Fotheringay Castle in 1587 she had survived by some years all the chief actors in the drama of Kirk o' Field.

It was, by any standard, a rash, brutal and clumsy enterprise. Yet the little groups of assassins, armed and cloaked, making their way, not too stealthily, through the streets and alleys of Edinburgh on a cold February night, played their squalid part in a vast turning movement in European history. The capital event in strategy was on a grander scale and was carried out with greater efficiency.

The Duke of Alva's Spanish army of 10,000 picked musketeers and cavalry, accompanied by 2000 picked prostitutes (also under iron discipline), marched northwards from Italy over Mont Cenis, through Savoy, Burgundy and Lorraine. It arrived in the Netherlands in August, about a month after Mary Stuart was shut up in Lochleven.

One student of events had no doubts about the longer-range significance of the presence of a Spanish army in Antwerp. Queen Elizabeth knew that danger to her throne and to Protestantism in England had moved a long march nearer. Spanish infantry in the Low Countries needed only Spanish galleys to bring them over the North Sea. In the late summer of 1567, the Counter-Reformation was, as the result of a single military movement, vastly strengthened as a presence and a menace.

There was only one minor score chalked up on the other side of the board, the elimination of the Catholic Queen of Scotland. And for this the chief credit must be given to the Calvinist zealots whose leader was John Knox. By their unsparing propaganda, they created a climate of opinion, especially in Edinburgh, which made it impossible for Mary to rule.

To achieve this purpose, prejudices were pitilessly sacrificed, fixed opinions were reversed: Lord Darnley, a dissolute young prince and a Papist at that, was transformed at a touch of the wand of necessity into a figure of infinite pathos, a martyr butchered by an adulterous spouse. Good Christian people were implored to do the Lord's work in bringing justice and vengeance upon his slayers. The well-thumbed pages of the Old Testament were scanned by expert eyes for admonitions that would fire the consciences and steel the hearts of the people against the Jezebel who was their lawful queen. So much energy, so much passion, so long sustained in a campaign of hatred.

Knox at least was sensitive to the new and precarious state of the Protestant cause in Europe brought about when Alva's 'agreeable and jolly army'[1] marched into Brussels. And, as he could, he responded to the danger.

By engineering the expulsion of Mary, he made it likely that, during the most critical years, Scotland would not be the base for a Catholic enterprise against England. When the English Catholic earls rose in the North, they got no succour from over the Border.

Elizabeth was left with the problem of Mary, formidable in all conscience, but easier to supervise as a captive, easier to spy on, and, if need be, to control. After all the anxiety that her dear sister sovereign had caused her—and would still cause her—one solid gain was left: the bright bird with the sharp claws had walked into the cage. The key to the cage was in Elizabeth's keeping. Hesitations and pretences and duplicities there would be. But the door would stay shut. The bird would never fly again.

1. Brantôme.

Appendix A

LETTER II	Crawford's account

He found great fault that I was
pensive. . . .

And then he said:
Ye ask me what I mean by the
cruelty contained in my letter?
It is of you alone that will not
accept my offers and repentance.

And moreover he said:
Ye asked me what I meant by
the cruelty specified in my
letters:
That proceedeth of you only,
that will not accept my offers
and repentance.

I confess that I have failed, but
not into which I have ever
denied; and siclike has failed too
sundry of your subjects which
you have forgiven.

I confess that I have failed in
something, and yet greater faults
have been made to you sundry
times, which you have forgiven.

I am young.
Ye will say that ye have forgiven me oft times, and yet that
I return to my faults. May not a
man of my age, for lack of
counsel fall twice or thrice or in
lack of his promise and at last
repent himself and be chastised
by experience?

I am but young, and ye will say
ye have forgiven me diverse
times.
May not a man of my age, for
lack of counsel, of which I am
very destitute, fall twice or
thrice, and yet repent and be
chastised by experience?

If I may obtain pardon I protest I shall never make fault again. And I crave no other thing but that we may be in bed and board together as husband and wife.

And if you will not consent hereunto, I shall never rise out of this bed.

I pray you tell me your resolution.

God knows how I am punished for making my god of you and for having no other thought but on you.
And if at any time I offend you, ye are the cause, because, when any offends me if for my refuge, I might plain unto you, I would speak it to no other body; but when I hear anything not being familiar with you, necessity constrains me to keep it in my breast, and that causes me to tyre my wit for very anger.
I answered aye to him but that would be overlong to write at length.
I asked why he would pass away in the English ship . . .

If I have made any fail that ye but think a fail, howsoever it be, I crave your pardon and protest that I shall never fail again.
I desire no other thing but that we may be together as man and wife.

And if you will not consent hereto, I desire never to rise forth of this bed.

Therefore I pray you, give me an answer hereunto.

God knoweth how I am punished for making my god of you, and for having no other thought but on you.
And if at any time I offend you, ye are the cause, for that when one offends, if for my refuge, I might open my mind to you, I would speak to no other; but when anything is spoken to me, and ye and I not being as husband and wife should be, necessity compelleth me to keep it in my breast, and bringeth me in such melancholy as ye see me in. She answered that it seemed true and she was sorry for his sickness, and she would find remedy therefore as soon as she might. She asked him why he would have passed away in the English ship . . .

He denies it and swears there-
unto; but he grants that he spake
with the men . . .
After this I inquired him of the
inquisition of Hiegait. He denies
the same, while I show him the
very words was spoken.
At which time he said that
Minto had advertised him, that
it was said that some of the
Council had brought a letter to
me to be subscrivit to put him
in prison and to slay him if he
made resistance. . . .

He answered that he had spoke
with the English man but not of
mind to go away with him.
And if he had, it had not been
without cause.
Then she asked him of the purpose of Higate, he answered
that it was told him.
She required how and by whom
it was told him.
He answered that the Laird of
Minto told him that a letter was
presented to her in Craigmillar
made by her own choice and
subscribed by certain others who
desired her to subscribe the
same, which she refused to
do. . . .

I had almost forgot that he said
he could not doubt of me in this
purpose of Hegart's for he
would never believe that I, who
was his proper flesh, would do
him any evil . . . But as to any
others that would pursue him at
least he should sell his life dear
enough but he suspected nobody.

And he said that he would never
think that she who was his own
proper flesh would do him any
hurt and if any other would do
it, they should buy it dear. . . .
Albeit he suspected none.

He would not let me depart
from him but desired that I did
wake with him.

So he desired her affectionately
to bear him company. For she
ever found some ado to draw
herself from him to her own
lodging . . . She was very pensive. Whereat he found fault.

He would very fain that I should lodge in his lodging. I refused it and said to him that he behoved to be purged and that could not be done here.

He said to me, I hear say that ye have brought a litter with you but I had rather have passed with you.

He was advertised she had brought a litter with her.
She answered that because she understood he was not able to ride on horseback she brought a litter that he might be carried more softly . . .

I answered that I wd take him with me to Craigmillar where the medicinar and I might help him and not be far from my son. He answered that he was ready when I pleased so I would assure him of his request.

She answered that she would take him to Craigmillar when she might be with him and not far from her son.
He answered that upon conditions he would go with her which was that he and she might be together at bed and board as husband and wife and that she should leave him no more.

Appendix B

For various reasons, modern statistical techniques which may have value in determining questions of authorship can only have a limited application to the Casket Letters. The techniques depend on the pattern of sentence-length and on the frequency with which certain simple words ('the', 'of', 'in', 'and', etc.) occur in a text. These factors in a doubtful passage are compared with what is found in a passage of established authorship. And deductions are drawn, with greater or less assurance.

But the Casket Letters are, it seems, translations from French originals which are (with the exception of one letter) unknown.

The length of sentences and the use of common words in the available texts could be influenced by the predilections of translator as well as by the mental habit of the author. Further, with what established texts of Mary's can the Letters be compared? A queen usually has secretaries at her elbow. She may dictate to them or amend drafts which they submit to her. The letters she signs are, in the ordinary way, joint productions. The Casket Letters, on the other hand, purport to be written by an individual.

Clearly then, it would be absurd to make exaggerated claims for the statistical method as offering a key to the Casket Letters. At most, it can strengthen or modify an impression that has already been formed on other evidence.

Stylistically, Letter III shows the greatest variation from the other finds in the famous silver-gilt casket. It is a carefully composed, elaborate and euphuistic fantasy, a conscious literary exercise. It is sent by the hand of Paris, once Bothwell's servant, later Mary's.

What can simple arithmetic add to the sense of the letter itself?

In the other seven letters, the average length of sentence is 23 words; in this one, it is 60; nearly three times as long. While, from its incidence in the other letters, we might expect 'of' to occur 15 times, it occurs 31 times; 'the' should appear 20 times and, in fact, appears 32 times; 'and' is present on 16 occasions and not the 22 that would be expected; 'in' occurs 14 times instead of 19. A substantial toll of discrepancies.

There is, however, one curious point of resemblance between Letters III and the long letter (II) from Glasgow. The writer of III says that she has sent a lock of her hair by Paris and the last sentence of the letter opens, 'I have shown unto this bearer that which I have learned, to whom I remit me, knowing the credit that you gave him'. In Letter II, Mary writes, 'Upon this point the bearer will show you many small things. Because I have overmuch to write and it is late. I give trust unto him upon your word'. The bearer of Letter II was probably Paris.

It is, of course, possible that two women, both in love with Bothwell, wrote in similar terms about one who was Bothwell's confidential servant. But the similarity of the two sentences strengthens the opinion that, in spite of the evidence of style and statistics, Letter III may be Mary's after all.

Letter V may be held suspect because the average length of its sentences (46 words) is well above the average of the group of letters as a whole, and above the average (32 words) of, say, the Queen's letter to Lord Burghley on September 9, 1571. But Letter V opens, 'My heart alas! Must the folly of a woman whose unfaithfulness to me you do sufficiently know', and Letter VI begins, 'Alas! My Lord why is your trust put in a person so unworthy'.

The impetus, the 'attack', of these two openings springs from the same mind. And Letter VI bears in one sentence the plain hallmark of Mary Stuart: 'To be short, he is all contrary.' The phrase which is known to be a translation of the French 'en somme', occurs twice in Letter VIII, and five times in Letter II.

The statistical evidence, such as it is, supports the opinion that the Casket Letters, with one possible exception, are products of the same pen, which can only be that of Mary Stuart.

It has been conjectured that Letter II was tampered with. Mr. Armstrong Davison considers that it was concocted from a letter to Bothwell and a letter to Moray, with interpolations supplied from a letter written to Bothwell by an unknown woman. All that need be said here is that statistical analysis of the Letter supplies no evidence of any process of inserting, patching or stitching.

Letters IV, VII and VIII are, on statistical as well as internal, evidence, the work of the writer of Letters I and II. They are, in other words, from the pen of Mary Stuart.

Bibliography

Accounts of the Lord Treasurer of Scotland, 1566–67. H.M. Register House (Edinburgh).

Anderson, James. *Collections Relating to the History of Mary, Queen of Scotland.* Fletcher Giles (London, 1729).

Bain, Joseph. *Calendar of Scottish Papers, 1563–1569.* H.M. Register House (Edinburgh, 1900).

Bourciez, Édouard. *Littérature de Cour sous Henri II.* Librairie Hachette (Paris, 1886).

Buchanan, George. *The Tyrannous Reign of Mary Stewart.* Ed. W. A. Gatherer. Edinburgh University Press (Edinburgh, 1958).

Calderwood, Alma B. *The Buik of the Kirk of the Canongait.* Scottish Record Society (Edinburgh, 1961).

Davison, M. H. Armstrong. *The Casket Letters.* University Press of Washington, D.C. (Washington, 1965).

Diurnal of Occurrents. Bannatyne Club. Volume 45. (Edinburgh, 1833.)

Edinburgh, Records of Burgh. Scottish Burgh Records Society (Edinburgh, 1875).

Evans, Joan. *A History of Jewellery, 1100–1870.* Faber and Faber (London, 1953).

Gore-Brown, Robert. *Lord Bothwell.* Collins (London, 1937).

Grant, I. F. *Social and Economic Development of Scotland.* Oliver and Boyd (Edinburgh, 1930).

Grant, James. *Old and New Edinburgh.* Cassell (London).

Henderson, T. F. *The Casket Letters.* A. and C. Black (Edinburgh, 1890).

Héritier, Jean. *Catherine de Medicis.* Libraire Arthème Fayard (Paris, 1959).

Herries, Lord. *Historie of the Reigne of Marie, Queen of Scots.* Abbotsford Club (Edinburgh, 1836).

Hume, Martin. *The Love Affairs of Mary, Queen of Scots.* Eveleigh Nash (London, 1903).

Illustrations of the Reign of Queen Mary. Maitland Club. Volume 25 (Glasgow, 1837).
Inventaires de la Royne Déscosse, Douairiere de France. Ed. Joseph Robertson. Bannatyne Club (Edinburgh, 1863).

Jenkins, Elizabeth. *Elizabeth the Great.* Gollancz (London, 1958).

Keith, Robert. *History of the Affairs of Church and State in Scotland.* Spottiswoode Society (Edinburgh, 1844–50).
Kerr, Henry F. Proceedings, Society of Antiquaries of Scotland, 1931. Page 140. For interpretation of drawing of Kirk o' Field.
Knox, John. *Historie of the Reformation.* Fleming (Edinburgh, 1732).

Labanoff, Prince Alexandre. *Lettres de Marie Stuart.* Charles Dolman (Londres, 1844).
Laing, Malcolm. *The History of Scotland.* Constable (Edinburgh, 1819).
Lang, Andrew. *The Mystery of Mary Stuart.* Longman, Green (London, 1901).
Law, Thomas Graves. Article, 'Mary Stewart'. *Cambridge Modern History,* Volume III. University Press (Cambridge, 1904).
Lee, Maurice. *James Stewart, Earl of Moray.* Columbia University Press (New York, 1953).
Lythe, S. G. E. *The Economy of Scotland.* Oliver and Boyd (London, 1960).

MacKenzie, Agnes Mure. *The Scotland of Queen Mary.* Maclehose (London, 1936).
Mahon, R. H. *The Tragedy of Kirk o' Field.* Cambridge University Press (Cambridge, 1920).
Melvil, Sir James. *Memoirs.* D. Wilson (London, 1752).
Muir, Edwin. *John Knox.* Cape (London, 1929).
Mumby, Frank A. *The Fall of Mary Stuart.* Constable (London, 1921).

Nau, Claude. *The History of Mary Stewart.* Ed. Jos. Stevenson, s.j. Paterson (Edinburgh, 1883).
Nogueres, Henri. *The Massacre of St. Bartholomew* (trans.). Allen and Unwin (London, 1902).
Norris, Herbert. *Costume and Fashion,* III. D. M. Dent and Sons (London, 1938).

Philippson, Martin. *Histoire du Regne de Marie Stuart*. Bouillon (Paris, 1891).

Phillips, James Emerson. *Images of a Queen*. University of California Press (Berkeley and Los Angeles, 1965).

Pitcairn, Robert. *Criminal Trials in Scotland*, Volume I. William Tait (Edinburgh, 1833).

Roeder, Ralph. *Catherine de' Medici and the Lost Revolution*. Harrap (London, 1937).

Russell, E. *Maitland of Lethington*. Nisbet (London, 1912).

Sitwell, Edith. *The Queens and the Hive*. Macmillan (London, 1962).

Teulet, A. *Lettres de Marie Stuart*. Didot (Paris, 1859).

Teulet, A. *Papiers d'État*. Tome Second. Plon (Paris).

Williams, H. Noel. *The Brood of False Lorraine*. Hutchinson (London, 1922).

Scottish Historical Review; *Dictionary of National Biography*; *The Complete Peerage*.

Index